AF604878

GREGORY DAY

SOUTH SIGHTED NESS

MELBOURNE, AUSTRALIA
www.transitlounge.com.au
Copyright © 2025 Gregory Day
First published 2025
Transit Lounge Publishing

This book is copyright. Apart from any fair dealing for the purpose of private study, research, criticism or review, as permitted under the Copyright Act, no part may be reproduced by any process without written permission. Inquiries should be made to the publisher.

Every effort has been made to contact all copyright holders. The publisher will be pleased to amend in any future editions any omissions brought to their attention.

Words and music by Paul McCartney
© Copyright MPL Communications Ltd

Cover design: Sian Marlow/Peter Lo
Typeset in 11/14pt Whitman by Cannon Typesetting

Printed in China by Everbest

A cataloguing-entry is available from
the National Library of Australia

ISBN: 978-1-923023-28-4

for TonTon, artist-gardener, great believer

The swift fire darting through a thunder cloud.
Dante, Paradiso

Sing the changes.
Paul McCartney

Contents

II

III

Little Marsh – an introduction

Herein lies a book of poems but the thing about this little marsh we live around is that you almost feel it should be free of books. By that I mean free of fixity, of permanent (mock permanent!) incisions, so that it's left to elude categories, to grow and tumble, to gather its reeds and tides under the governing motion of the moon, sun and stars.

And yet, so often it is the books that remind us of this movement, the way they express with ink and paper what we see and feel around us, and what we hear: the thrumming of quail wings, the language of raintap on padded leaf, the tourist buses, and always the ocean.

We need those books that do not capture but release – a near miraculous act – books that celebrate not just mentally, emotionally, optically, sonically, but in-the-round and elementally, from that, yes, eternal impulse to sing and say.

To sing and say with the heart's mind, in the solitude surrounding the union between the reader and what is read. Perhaps by the fire, perhaps in the garden, perhaps even in the middle of maelstrom and chaos.

Wherever there is time, time beyond time.

To sing, to say, to write – in terms of being human these are all ways.

Moments come and go like sunshowers, shining with passing light, proving that we do have the desire to share and remember.

I

And When I Woke

Mainly sky the photo was and when I woke
the light had taken two thirds of my mind
and when I walked out on russet flats
the birds were now a silky kin like souls
emerged from paintings past or psalms
to radiate the scene. They were discredited spirits
feathered again with happinesses against the cold
streaming in the hi-tech air, brushing
smiles onto my lips, tapping my eyes with
lightblue flight and the sun-bucklings of pools.
With the whole world inside my body I turned
a bend in the river, found a dwelling place,
lay down between wild root and cultivated frond
counted the nights I'd slept without such dreams
closed my eyes and ceased to count them anymore.

The Subtle Track of the Wallaby Mind

I think and then think differently. I think differently then I think again and so to not think at all, or better, to run on numberless sticks in light, infinite wires of grass *my skeletons my bones* eternal hairy leaves *my gall my kidney stones* a myriad sundew stars *continual crosses & pietas*, I scamp toward the source, I bound like a surrealist, unbind like foam of the creek, I stop in spate not to think again but to chew on stillness.

Perhaps it's then, feeling so perfectly at home, that I spill the tannin creek down my belly-front? But who keeps sprinkling rust onto my nape as I look down?

Impossible Life

I saw him this morning
with his newspaper under his arm
the sadness under his eyes.
The nights have been stormy
the days all blue & fresh
but if what they say is true
he never walks the tides anymore
he's given up on the bush tracks
they never see him in the pub.
He stays at home alone, his brickhome
the phases of the moon over his bed,
cuttlefish bones and sponges on his sills,
the TV taking pride of place
in the living room with the Douglas fir walls.
Thinking back it's only taken four years
from the moment he described, in a rush of grinning,
how he decided to *shove it all*,
shove the traffic and the frenetics,
the parking officers and the *druggies*,
and move like an actress to a coastal town.
Initially he'd call it a *village*
his house was a *cottage*,
something resembling a red-rooved child's story
with gables & chimneys
and seagulls with names.

And so it was that he tied up his loose ends,
telephoned his kids, one in Yarraville, one in Balwyn
to tell of the charming little place he thought he could love
a place that he could flower in

with it's quirky & supportive community all around him.
It was an impossible life
and now after the slow decay of such fiction
an expressionless routine has taken its place.

The shore looks empty of love or mythologies
the bush looks rattled & drab
the faces at the store wear smiles of misunderstanding.

An impossible life, like heaven
or superstardom, a bird's life
and now he knows it.
He has disengaged from the Community Hall Committee,
no longer raises ethics to the local paper
he finds the countermeal prices too exy
and the post office box too often empty.
What do those guys talk about in the surf? he asks himself,
they never seem to have very much to say to me.
And what about the infernal changing of the wind
this weather that has no reassurance.

It must've dawned on him (and possibly at dawn,
with his moons on the wall glazed in easterly pink)
that he was a digit in a migration-demographic,
that he had given away what he knew
for what desire dreamt he could possibly be.
The flower of his idea, cut off
from its stock as it was, had died
in the reality of soil and growing conditions
leaving him feeling gratuitious

any illusion of landedness or camaraderie gone
and everything around him moving undertaker-slow
the nights entrenched in P.D.James
and the TV his only continuity.

Possum Lace

We make no lace in this district
nothing to honour the dressers with,

there's only grass or lace of silver rain
coastal porphyry or blue-gray basalt plain.

What came before us is still incised on possum skins
together with song & thread

then buried in dignity with the dead.
But now possums running free on our wires

are seldom seen as sacred. We're left undecorated
with no whole community rituals to celebrate nature and the soul.

Heathpack

The birds live a parallel existence to us in this place.
Their comings and goings.
Chords and clusters.

Three pelicans flying past the Moriac Store.
A skein of ibis over the nutbrown paddocks.
The nimble swallows tousling the dunes.

Fourteen swans arrive to glide the inlet for three days
in the midweek.
By Saturday they're gone to a place no google-earther knows,
some soak of metaphysical reeds beyond coordinates.

A brown wren bounces on the tongue of cliff
triggering the voice in my head. The cadence rises,
a glowing-white gannet in the Picasso-blue of late afternoon.

The night to come has got into the colour of the sea,
some of the earth too, the way soil seeds the clouds.
Time is music then, the wren has found its pair

to dinner-dance amid the ocean sound.
Above what precise patch of moonah-loam will they sleep tonight?
In what proximity to the bristlebird?

It behooves us not to know
we haven't made it impossible for them just yet.
So yes, let's say that's joy they're tweeting in the evening light

the indispensable song of right-place-right-time
our language might call Life. They do compute and metaphor
but too quick to scribble down or Excel.

Life for all then, private, an untrackable symphony,
no notation of wood or wind, no emulsion even
but what's stored in the battery of the heath, in the sea-bed.

Now the swell is coming on, gesturing towards the cliffs
before surging through the guzzle-clefts. As night descends
the place is light, made of light - ask the planets watching on

where every dawn's an anniversary
ask the birds but just for fun
content in the knowledge you may never get an answer.

In Country Victoria

for Peter Temple

Just like another powerless person in polar fleece
living outside the zone of influence & legitimate thought
taking cues from nature, characters of the weather,
applying the lessons as law onto current events
rather than skulling the menu in a team-suburb:
it's a type of new pastorale, a mind's free field
refilched, thinking through bends in a clear stream
with, it has to be said, a romance that visitors will arrive.
But it's so invisible, as numerous & hidden as circuit boards:
take the freeway exit ramp, drive west, cross the railway
and follow the cypress windbreaks till the grey letterbox
like in crime fiction, where the independence is criminal,
being innocent is sneaky, and critical's just another rainy day.

Squall

You can't undo a squall
gusting over the strait
thrumming through the eye of the needle
belting then rusting the headlands.

The house is a stay but for how long?
Fees are piling up
scattering tea-tree down
salt air stinging in the wounds.

Climate a mirror of existence you say?
A mentor of the mind?
The sky no cosy club the earth no saving god
the wind no soothing word?

Plastic as colonisation the weather
walls a past demolished
forecasting no barometers if finally
all this will peter out, cease to be…

Sister Light

Wind braids the grass & combs the hides
of herefords standing or reclining in clods.
In the foreshortening view rusted rivertrees
with pines create a welcome belt.
Under the bruised sky over the metal road
farm fencewires zing, guitars hang on silent nails.
The rain tunes out and in, greening single bowsers,
printing the world with tattoos of weather.
Rounding a long bend, eyelids almost touching
I see a light-filled wetland, peering through the glare.
Adrift in the glitter, windscreen shining
I hear an ancient chorus singing in the sky.
Suddenly I'm in yearning, for my sister to come back
to tour with me at last these swan-dotted soaks.
The birds sound her return and my eyes
swing from the road toward the centre of their song.
The whole wetland fills, tilts on its side, pours open
drenching the empty passenger seat in light.

Natural Pain

The magpie from beyond the plastic curtains
winding her song like dawn through the leaves.
The hare beyond the chink of brightness
a rufous omen across the hospital slope.

Swift as flight the pair of them, ears pricked up
Do you think you'll come right? I asked,
watching the TV stock-market ribbon from his bed.
I wouldn't have thought so, he said.

He plunged to new lows then, death's lights, before rising
again to us and the grandchildren on his lap.
They heard the bird just as speech left him
his sounds became animal, a new dawn in the offing.

Will we inject him? we asked.
He eyed us like executioners of twilight
misinterpreting natural pain, his song of dying.
So where are you going to now? I cried

only hours after he had finally gone.
The colour not of his corpse but of the hare
the blinding light of the warbling bird
made his ringing non-reply.

Toíbín's Cush

The silverfish-eaten edges of the cover of *The Heather Blazing*
look like this: the book has lived, the teeth of time's community
have eroded its presentation yet thickened its setting in Cush.

As I open the novel my fading signature tells me how
time dispenses with us and our books in riparian ways.
The river runs both swift and slow, it streams and it pools

and as the edges of the cover show, it nibbles at all
our painterly banks. The signature's in black-ink gone eel-brown
and is actually dated: *Spring. 93*. So there it is: *The Heather Blazing*

is also a spring, a source migrating (like the eels, like the beam
from the lighthouse at Tuskar Rock on pg. 9) always issuing
along genetic flows where novels travel like Dwyers

through our family veins to this other lighthouse beam,
at Split Point facing Tasmania, its keeper's cottage insulated
with a seaweed pith against southwesterlies.

This doubling book then, of deckled cliff and timbercrash,
this other Toíbín's Cush. It's simply the rain refilling the river,
polishing the sand and its lenses, all of which will end up in the sea.

Bluetongue

Here astride the stile of class I wince not
for the loss of latin names but for the lizards
SUV flattened, tossed in plumes of road flour
yet uneaten. Those bluetongues we used to train
and dissect on school holidays not knowing latin names
nor how they would enter our hearts by killing them so
flattened in the digital scree, cryovacked before sixteen
the unclassifiable heart renaming the lizard a soulmate
for life or what it used to be. Here astride the habitat
is silent no grass or beak the jeeps black as tarmac
I sleep as if between the tyre and the road dreaming.

The Permeable Game

The freedom of his style was great
The way he spread from flank to flank
Then burst through the guts like the pent-up still
they used to coax on Delaney's corner.
With pluck like that he'd pick the lock of the pack
crumb then drill the nut to the blue-black end
the clouds massing west behind goalposts glowing white
– egrets in the dairymen's lactating light –
with the crowd by the kiosk rising to their feet.
In a gully northeast of the oval the molten creek
was a welder's flux winding in concert with his game,
from contest to contest through silage and bracken
his effect was hydraulic his legs stout mannagums his lungs
volcanic lakes his eyes the trout of apparition on the skin
of the whiskey creek. He read the ball like soil on local tongues
before long the whole team was on its racing bike, leaning
into rainslick bends, belting down old blackwood swales,
they piled on goal after goal with spokeflashing brilliance,
their cohesion gathering like cockies around grain, their teamwork
a Celtic lace on ancestral muscles come to clear a farm and box-on.
The other mob were felled like first timber
Ringbarked, grubbed and chained, flung and burnt
in a rooted heap right there on the twilit sward.
Such is the smoking smell of success in these winter dusks
The secret punishing victories that lead us off into the night
To gather verses in a moonlight left by heroes.

Frogs

In running water over grass
rose-gold glitz and neon linings
tadpoles festooning
quicksilvered with glamour
& plump belly-lamp light.
When innocence is shucked
for fresh legs and a voice
life leaps diaphanous into the flowing braid.
If we go down close, ear to the ditches
green blades tickle our lobes
our eyes wetten with wonder
our nose fills with creation
senses reunited
in the festival of new frogs.

Grey Hair

By candlelight of mid-morning
my brothers' hair is grey
falling straight as wood
beside their daylit faces.

My brothers are Dwyers and Days
Hegartys and Denerios and Coopers
once they smelt of hay and euchre
they smell now of saltwater

Prayers of the past
descending like the grey hair
also other lines, of other prayers
from Kerala, Balian, the city temples.

Where we listened once
in the Earl of Ormond's garden
to his high orders from neurotic windows
we're now floating free in the memory

Gathered in an empty beach house
loosely sifting pages from a book of sand
presenting morning tea to our startling grandma
reciting sailors' poems from another shore.

Middlemarch

Midweek, Grassy Creek
she reads *Middlemarch* in the waves

her gaze cretaceous
water marbles

characters thinking
in deep pools

before editing
to shallow destinations.

Her ankles frill
she steps from the last page

Her finely-touched spirit, its fine tissues
enveloped by the residue

which has no great name
on the earth, receding

like all written texts into
the ocean roar.

The Old Regime

Sedge grass, xanthorrhea
and messmate woolly-limbed
from regrowth after fire

dusk light on the knolled
auditoria of flicker-flack
the media of wing-frisk

& wattlebird thwack
above grass-tree menhirs
inciting frond-splay

purveyors of air
whose beauty is clear film
over hill-lines, leaf-clouds

visible from *the other side*
the world a vast vitrine
of dreaming water-walls

& heath-lined skink-silver
tracks flowing eelwards
everyday, winding upwards

to a blue milk of stars
where banksia-babes & sheoak bubs
fall as flowerspikes and filaments

of the old regime
the everlastingness evident
on one rounded hill

late light on its page
of wood-ash-soil, its scribbly life
prickle-shy, with nibs of sharp

conebush, & salt
we could list for hours
it's not a forgotten heart

it lives
in this hour beyond breaches
a tableau of distant waves

hitting
the last point
before the bay's shelter

where the hills collect
gliders, grains,
quolls, vistas

of dwelling sight
a gloaming height
with heath for crown

the inflorescence
of a sky upshedding
a slowtapping sap-dance

wrought naturally
into boats of cloud
clouds afloat

fleece across star over reef
punctuating
the new demesne.

Billy

We'll fill the billy with imagery
Where once we filled it with tea
And we'll swat flies & shield our eyes
Not from the sun but the set lights.

Once a troupe of vaudevillians
Traipsed from show to canvas show through here
Saw the camber of a hardwood stump
Read the initials in the tree.
One bright accordion even wrote a song about it
Which they all sang drunk by the Barwon.
Now they've laid out a long white table
And brought a comedian & a cartoonist for a *yarn*.
They're shooting the scene in 'Bill Peach black & white'
And no-one's to piss near the make-up tree.

Might frighten the ants I suppose.

The Sound Of Thuds

What does the wallaby see through her eyes
when she chances upon me at the edge of the clearing?
She stops, waits....her open ears like
the turned-around vertical eyes of a cat.
Her whole head looks.
The shock sends her swivelling

briefly scrambling
on the proverbial threepenny bit
in the dirt and leaf litter before bounding off
into the currency of well-gullied messmates.

So, what does she see? A shape, dark outline,
an opaque scale big enough to warn? Or firesticks
and spears, grass burning, dingos gnashing?
Or, well breeched squatters, naturalists,
doyens of the land grab and the Henri-Martini rifle,
come to take her soul, her souls
as specimens, as livelihoods, as imperial right?

The sound of the thuds in the silver soiled gully
is briefly like a man being punched.
Then it is the sound of speed, of ground swallowed up,
a bass contact between paw and swale
with a crinkle of dried leaves flying.

The flamming thud disappears on its way.
The bush goes silent.
An unnerving breeze passes over
an imaginary creek in the trees
Binding the moment.

Corangamite

What I'm seeking from these stone walls mantling
the richsoiled rises is not my father
but a bird from his time and place, a lake
for the bird to woo upon, a hope
I can countenance in a bleakening world.
Watching these lava rocks cool before us
is like chasing thermals without wings
instead a lichened GPS for the old blue Renault
meandering over hummock and hillock for brolgas.
The grass-heads wave, a bone calls immortal
I'm not weeping I've wept and the windscreen
is what I'm left with: an eye for connections
looking for flocks rather than individuality,
a stilt-legged dinner-dance on a replenished lake.

Milkskin Caul

When God is described as an idea
Poems are layed aslant on drawing boards
Exhibited with their feet turned up
Like the wax-paper plans of dead buildings

When furniture becomes fire rather than function
And food becomes a milkskin caul
From 'Nature's Replete Boutique'
It's time to skip lunch
And head for the funny mirrors in the museum*.

** A little wan, nevertheless the spirit is lean, and this mixed with the laughter in front of the mirrors restores the balance. We are exhibits in this comedy, in our voluminousity and stretch, all our exaggeration. The outing of our absurdity comes as a great relief.*

Tourist Town

That day when Q went into the water
The world was not torn, he did not have diaorrhea
Not dizziness on the steps, nor liver or glandular pain.
As he stood there in the unroaring surf
With his back to the container ship on the horizon
Looking at the cliffs and the houses capping them
He felt a memory like a bristlebird disappearing inside of him.
The water seemed suddenly rooved by the summer's mind
Which expanded in what to him seemed a vascular way
Sucking in free air and putting out posture
Or *good cheer*. As he turned he couldn't help but judge
And infect the waves: monotonic, mechanistic, calibrated even.
He wanted just the simple dream of girls and getting well
But stood instead like a too-bright ghost
Yearning for the obscurity of winter.

Ecological Line

Trace that ecological line
From Achilles & Ulysses to here.
See how the high triremes ruled the waves
And how the horse got into Troy.
Roam out onto the margins of empire
To Etna, or the spring of Arethusa,
To the campagna & promontories
Above the sea on the Ionian instep.
Ask the ghosts of the beeches & birdless air
What happened there to haunt the world
With a dark and barren absence.
Ask the people where the plunder is,
The jewel-encrusted wedding-feasts,
The flowing golden bowls on plinths,
The chanting perlustration of the victories
We've never ceased to hear about.
(O the greatest thing a triumph has
Is an immortal poet to sing of it
No matter how the blow was struck!
No matter how the goblets got their wine!)

Across the parched *fiumare* flies
a wilderness of empty winds
that comb the land where forests stood
and brush the moisture from the clay.
There was so much leaf-face in Homer's day
He could've wrapped himself & slept in it
On nights when the starlight was full
And an easy warmth filtered through.
And with the leaves of course came rain

And trees & rain gave a balanced world,
Where rivers were the talisman
And not some piece of stolen eastern jade
stored tight under a breastplate.
They say a thousand rivers flowed
From mountainsides so steeped in trees
You could hear the currents in the breeze,
But now of course to scratch the soil
Where luscious roots once made a filigree
Is to come up hurt, bereft and bleeding
The whole alluvia rendered mythless and tired.

Password Mologa

Upon a pile of rocks we drove up in a gas-producing car burning redgum chips
to get the six wheels moving.
Quartz reflects whatever the sky decrees if the angle's right you catch the jottings of light
the whole cast-off world twinkles
Then the road's a starry track, to travel is to view fallen constellations and in your ear
a secret password is happily passed – *Mologa*

Later in the evening of the Victoria Hotel after sherberts and steak that word
becomes a plaything, *Go Mologi!*
As if there's more than one heartland or the place has become a man called that
the heart of home personified
Or as if we're cheering for the lost bond we share, to always risk the game of life and love,
and risk forever more.

My two young boys, oblivious inheritors, go to sleep in an upstairs room above the train line
remarking how cosy the world has become
Knowing nothing of the days of humiliation, the thistle-kickin' 1870s when their ancestors
spent as much time scrawling copperplate pleas
To the Lands Dept as they did scratching between white box and terrick pine for a quid.

But so it is hidden, pain is a code
most everything's gone and forgotten, been gone for decades since time's axle broke and
Uncle Bernie rode his bicycle
With the huge seat to pick the city cousins up from the red train.
The secret password
is seized upon, a lost postcode, in times like these
Mologa, Mologi, with a more demonstrative thumbs-up for who we are and will always be
and a glint in the smiling eye just like the quartz

that makes this heartland dance. On the edge of town, at the ant-teeming extent
of a cross-hatched scrap of civilization
The granite pyramid stands and remains a pure motif
in the changing sky.
In this scape of insignificances it is irony's painterly rise
You can never get lost with such a pointed reference to the flatness of the world
never lose your bearings, not here

Not on these celestial roads where once we scored the bushels, hoed the cream, recited
the Furphy-cart quatrain and cheered for rain.
We're cheering still, as this morning's early sky is bruised with it.
Slowly like an old rag squeeezed the drops of memory begin to clang on the hotel roof,

we swoon quietly inside for the connection, the square-mile blocks
that bind us,
the tears irrigating the dry canals of *Mologa*: our old home ground.

Lighting-up

Heath of wallaby fur
    unnegotiable by dog
              or camera
beside gnarled & mythic messmate
personages writhing
            where wind belts
out of the sea southwest
a marauding invader
  tearing
at the deckle-edge of the land.

This comes to mind
      in the day's last light
a sandygold of dozing tracks
      lit up like plot-points
    by the sun's readerly angle.

Hunting concerns scatter
       with impending starlight
the time for cultural play returns
      a dark screen of all past dramas
wheeling now toward us
    as the sun lowers its gaze
on material concerns.

Constant is the sound of the sea
    blood in the ears
        the senses perceiving
changing too with that slant gloaming –
in true night we hear shorebreak

in the campfire
harmonics in the starry eaves
and rivermouths gushed open
by tilting seas

By day these dynamics lessen
eyes displace ears
the fruit of sight is bitten into
supplanting the snap of nightwater
on dreaming sands.

This mobile proscenium
this cloud-theatre, this firemare
and granular curve of place.
Looking for the lighting-up
we walk transitional zones
between sea & cliff day & night
seeking buoyancies
prints embossed on
the
rose-gold track
of those who sang
before us.

Surfcoast Poem

opponents of home
go touring
into others
demanding service
getting lost

those with soul-places
become hosts
morning and night
the beach and hills
grow sad

performance rules
cockatoos glut
in wheelie-bins,
dialects = signage, love
spills from the bowser

Landbody Suite

1. En Pointe

'The coming of the dew' descends from a wise creative time, it sounds antique yet quietly in autumn's weakening sun it soothes our anxious brows.

After human summer thrusts have uploaded, 'go home' the sea exhales. It's then those gleamy beads of dew perform their ballet-on-grass-tips, taking their place *en pointe*: a million sighs of wind dancing dry dust into a cool moisture-song of space.

Thus the dew returns from a place beyond print, beyond description, and from a time before a language was created to fake the world as a light with no source.

Things get made, are found, leaves *turn*: the sun projects its beam through large windows, breezes feather the curtains, floorboards creak in knots & grains, our flesh and mud blood and grass in sheer velocity we seek by running, swimming, flying, drawing, writing.

We find our solution winking after all in deliquescent poise, in the passing mother-touch of dew.

2. A Sentence is a Wave Breaking from Left to Right

A sentence is a wave breaking from left to right
A wave breaking, a thought appearing from deep
in the cold ocean of your heart. Somewhere south
where the future brews, silent ice cedes to water
the world gathers its eyes, excitement gathers too,
a slow gulf of darkness waxing towards full disclosure
a hammered sliver breaking among starry mysteries
cooeeing to the earth's looking waters, which stir
towards sound like roe in the sassiest conditions.
And so, the skin of things is moved alive it furls
then builds it rises until suddenly a dolphin-leap
of language traces grammar in the air. Whatever
had been dwelling there, a bunched muscle, a lunar inkling,
a glimmer of reason, or a reason to sing, awakens.
The swell of becoming breaks into a foaming momentum
and – *there it is* – a sentence is formed.

3. Blossom

Evolution lit our fire on the beach and we threw our words onto it.

willow
pastorale
ambition

Inclined towards the sea we'd crawled through a sinkholy history where wolves founded cities and weather enacted its own ethical judgement. The gavels of this law were landslips thudding into previously livable coves, a section of modified woodland for instance, a whole modified woodland sea-cliff edge (once grassy woodland sea-cliff edge) biscuiting down to mingle with kelp and other leathery myths.

We exiled ourselves there, within the intertidal zone of reality and the imagination. Ideas came through the caves to where our speech was windblent. Any tired old words crackled and spat, resisting the pyre before surrendering to turquoise, then to the softest, most ceremonial ash.

So it was that stars fell like songs, lighting new horizons. We sat unstitching old textbooks, muscling Romulus and Remus, inciting blossom-inspirations of how to make our being land, like that plummeted bight, that collapsed promontory of weedy parrot-bush and moonah-reef now singing with the sands.

Burn, the night sang, burn sang the sands, burn the fallen woodland, burn like the changing colours, burn like 1750, burn like all the 1750s to come, burn to a blazing star the choking wattle-copse of your mind…

4. Face is Place

The back-country of a face, dwells like an ancient night, where curtains rise on a theatre of rocks and distant surf.

We don't have time we have change. Words exceed their limit as drudge grammatical currency to become the things they are, things of earth, a word a rock sung in that ancient night behind the face we offer to days.

And to the smallest birds we bring pasts presents barrel-dwelling philosophers and tomorrows, all the lights and sisterings of night, an open cave deep & opaque, a rivertop where tree-reflections play.

When we are full of the hope of birds we are also wanting to be that full. Our Orpheus our rock-word sings of how the cross of our sadness wheels, how it slowly turns in the south, its pointers dripping dew, grassing and reeding the ground with the life our masks have stolen, knowing *he is no hero who never met the dragon, or who, if he once saw it, declared afterwards that he saw nothing.*

Both when and where we die will be this ancient night of sunlit now, and hopefully, like the fighting Gunditjmara returning home to where the lava flows have cooled, we will leave the right spaces for readers of all the nights to come.

5. Headland

Headland headland after headland between headland headland waving trees headland bright sea-bite headland horizon reaching the headland hawkfall headland posted cormorant-monsignor headland fluttering-shirt swig headland sheep then headland that headland interpretation headland after school before school late for school headland rip headland word headland on headland slip headland another headland nyurru nyurru headland tour bewilder headland what? headland bluetongue-honeymoon once upon a fog headland starfall from the ship headland morning-dew headland monet mulcher headland itch stitch headland bristlebird headland underneath the headland past lost headland proud headland smiling descending steps headland edge headland where the car went over headland auction headland between the ears headland crumbling headland remember in the nostrils headland wagging school on the headland dogs headland sap headland thrip headland sheer swifts headland risk-assessment dear headland sibilance of headland brown bandicoot headland campfire headphones saidhead headland

6. Hospitality to Priests

At the heart of the whirlwind is a clear universal language
To learn the grammar of the stars among the plummeting mass
He stands out in the snow, his very hunger an offering
All you can do is prepare a corner somewhere, some
bread and beans.

But the whole landscape is teeming with requirements
Camps, illness, despair, we need a prayer for this
and thus we need a priest? He is the one
who has left the world while remaining among us

He is the one who can point out the constellations
the millions of spirits and how we are one
He is also the one who needs shelter and home cooking
when all seems exposed and nothing seems to grow.

Speak with him, speak of your poverty and injury,
Speak for velocity, and of grace. Before you turn him away
think of how one act of kindness keeps the world on its axis
How one act of ignorance destroys the family home.

7. My Offline Body

Codes are not dreams acronyms are not friends
I reach out to touch you but hello

this glitch is only curable
when we're camping in groundcovers

when birdsong becomes lexicon a muse inspired
by clarifications of a Greek chorus

a village shown to itself, sung and soared.
We keep coming back to wetland soaks

ephemeral but significant as humans or news
which lasts as long as solstice dew

a city of elapsing life or singed wings
of butterfly hearts journeying.

By fire after fire risking hopes of connection
I want to see you but

you are gone, I want to touch you yet
I might mark the screen.

8. Crossroads

On an old chair in the mind nature was waiting patiently for all distraction to end. Nothing always makes sense to eagles flying over, what you see are marks on the land what they see are groundlarks. She lands with full span by that crosshaired crossroads, looks askance at the tree, stands tall next to the chair. Eagle, resident of the mind. The branches whisper nervously but it is the tree that begins to speak.

'Today,' the tree says, 'is like no-other day. My leaves are 1000 faces, my branches are routes to heaven, my sap is impeccable fuel. All who pass by this way must benefit, and all are encouraged to make an offering. All proceeds will go to funding Madame Eagle here on the journey to reclaim her rightful crown.'

A travelling band is passing by. Their air is civil war. They have had a big night, think they have heard it all, but this is bigger. A clarinet descends, a bassoon lands. A gnawing hunger falls on the players until, finally, they are quiet. Now there is wind, wind in the grasses, in which the groundlarks too are still.

Finally, the eagle spreads her wings. The breeze pirouettes. One by one the band come forward, to play their reedy currency, at that unticketed crossroads. The bird is lifted aloft on the sound, and flies again to that sacred place from which the world is set in motion.

9. Keepsakes Are Common But Wind Changes Are More Frequent

for Sian

Round about now is when I peer through the foilage, but
are you there?
Whenever I'm lost I remember my childhood, why is that?
Everytime I look in the mirror I hear an echo, is that normal?
God made the world and all its disasters, but you make
the marmalade.

Is that calligraphy or bracken on your mind?
Are you looking at me, or at the sea behind me?
Is that local gossip interrupting your silence?
Do you want your ideas to be buried or cremated?

Keepsakes are common but wind changes are more frequent.
The ear is to the eye what blossom is to the clifftop.
It is possible to have more opinions than feelings.
Sleep is a landscape like work is a boat.

When you cry you're not here, so surely you're in the trees.
If my childhood was lost then who is this adult who found me?
Sometimes it's wattlebirds, sometimes the ocean.
There's nothing like tea & toast alone with you in autumn.

10. Rainy Routes. 1942.

Wanting to know how difficult or easy it was to find freedom she was shown three possibilities: a rainy windowpane, a crisscrossed pasture of cows, and an oak tree scribbled on by termites. She was given the choice.

The stench of drying dung in a childhood drought she kept at bay. She also withstood the termites eating their way through precious libraries of the forest. In the end her fondest memories of winter won, she chose the soft wistfulness of the rainy pane.

But look, her guide said, pointing at the window. Look at the blunt tracks of our desires, the way the world displays them there. Look too at how everything is falling, like tears down the countryside of your face. Remember the pattern of those tears. They are the routes by which you'll get over the alps and into the free zone.

The guide assured her that although climbing falling water is difficult it had been done. St John of Chrysostom did it. Also the two Thereses. Look at it this way, he said. Then that way. If it was as simple as turning the world upside down and shaking it then we would already have found what we've lost. Each silver thread, each wet diversion, every scrambling roe you chase off into the trees could be your downfall. Your betrayer.

My advice, he said, is to start the journey as if you are already at the summit. Admire the view, the angels will sing. Remember too, there'll be no audit. For the mountain of rain to exist you only have to imagine it. It will tremble, it will fibrillate, and you will fall newborn into a waking world.

11. Allegory of the Figurine

Tuscany, 1321. Rifling through the soldier's tunic after he had been slain they found a small figurine (prefiguring Pinocchio), a vellum scrap of Lucretius's *On The Nature of Things* (prefiguring Bracciolini), a sprig of Cretan dittany (prefiguring Jamie Oliver), a stitched cylinder made from the stomach lining of a goat (prefiguring a condom), and a brief letter from the soldier's mother in Palermo (prefiguring a text message).

These objects the museum has pocketed loom larger than all the canyons of time between us. Nearly eight centuries collapse into just five keepsakes.

What really gets us thinking though is the allegory of the figurine. A wooden doll (made from an extinct subspecies of beech) whose long nose sniffs out eternity's lie. Lucretius' words, seriffing in sepia (cuttlefish ink) across the vellum scrap, only verify the irony. He writes that all life is predictable except the odd random event. It is this event which secures our enchantment. For instance, how is it, after all these centuries, that we can still smell the dittany? It's as if, in the end, only herbs, and not the curated intimacies of medieval soldiers, are immortal. I wonder then if the goatskin sheaf was a chafing apparatus, if he'd ever thought of slipping it over Pinocchio's nose.

Ultimately though, it's the mother's letter which touches our hearts. It *pings* through the years, we feel time screening backwards, the man becoming the boy, the beloved *bambino*.

So here we stand, Pinocchios all, looming over the time-space continuum. Is it the nature of reality that each time our nose grows the universe does too?

12. Return

We set off on the journey but when our hair becomes myrtle leaves our ears the mountain we screech like *djirnap* for it to stop.

Transformation is more than unexpected mail more than change it is *changing*.

Harry the verb all you like but lose the special effects, a more impressive technology would be one that could be still.

Instead wombats damage the moon fish come out of the dunes the town's an ashtray always being emptied and refilled.

Even the horizon is morphing the low hills on the chapel ceiling the dolphin leaping on your grandfather's signet ring now arriving to be kissed.

When we walk we leave behind when we leave behind we're missed when we arrive we sponge the messmate's limbs our worries soluble among the sundew.

The track's a rich vein for corporate seminars too but comes with a finely printed precipice.

Fall off, feel the eight centuries since the priest left the world walking alone through a snow laden field.

That's you in mid-air, gone over the edge, trees foresting your skull, your brain granite-black your heart a returning orphan finally at rest in its carriage.

II

Skiffleboard Judgement

a tin court, in the bosky lee, monday mid-morning session:

All rise!, the heron cries.

The judge presides. Opens his beak.

Be seated. Good Day to you all. Please observe the rules of the court. Present the defendant please.

A middle aged man in polo shirt and threequarter pants is ushered in.

So now, begins the judge. Is your name Mr Bradley Stephen Knew?

Yes, your honour.

And do you, Mr Knew, live by the sea?

Yes, your honour.

And do you call this body of water you live besides 'the sea'?

We call it that, sir.

And do you also call it 'the ocean', 'the water', 'the beach', 'the surf', 'the green sink,' 'the boat's tablecloth' etc...

Well, we do call it some of those things your honour.

What is a yawl, Mr Knew? Can the defendant define a

'yawl' for me please?

Silence in the court.

Well? Mr.Knew?

I cannot your honour. Unless maybe it is some kind of old tool.

Very well. Then have you any idea what a pinnace is?

Silence in the court. Apart from the muffled cluck of a small gull, the stenographer. She knows where this is headed.

No sir.

What are the common everyday uses of kelp, Mr Knew?

The defendant now looks about the court in some confusion. Glances at a friend in the public gallery who is reading the paper and refuses to communicate any expression in response.

Well, I know the Japanese eat seaweed sir.

Yes. Snaps the Judge. But what do *you* use it for? What do the people you are acquainted with use it for?

A penny drops inside Mr Knew.

Ah, he says. It's against the law to use it sir.

Very well. Then what's a neap tide?

A what, sir?

A neap tide Mr Knew. A NEAP tide.

It rings a bell.

Ah, it has something to do with the tides sir. I learnt that in school. Ah....

Do you live by the ocean Mr Knew?

Yessir.

(This said with what the gull-stenographer is sure is a cadence from the other side of the Pacific. She clucks.)

And so you live by the great teacher, the great relief and assassin?

I'm sorry, I don't understand.

Did you know that there are as many stars in our universe as there are grains of sand on the beach?

Ah, I kind of did know that, your honour.

How do you like to cook abalone?

I don't sir.

You don't like to cook abalone? You prefer it raw with a greek dip?

No sir. I have never eaten abalone.

I see. At what time of year do you observe whiting in the waters near your home?

I'm not sure, sir?

Well then, what type of paint did you use on your recently upgraded bathroom walls. I'm led to believe you enjoy the domestic arts, Mr Knew?

Porter's paint sir. Flame tree red.

Very good. Can you tell me why the raven appears on
the dune shrubbery of your inlet in January, and in large numbers?

I dunno.

You say you live beside the boat's tablecloth?

I'm sorry, sir?

What does a glass of Pinot Noir cost at your local cafe?

$12.50, your honour.

And on what day is your rubbish collected?

Tuesdays, sir.

So if a glass of Pinot Noir costs $12.50 at your local cafe and your rubbish is collected on tuesdays then it follows that you should know how many songs you can download onto your digital device?

Mr Knew giggles.

Is there something we should be amused at Mr Knew?

No, your honour?

So then, how many songs?

10,000 sir.

The judge looks down and shuffles some paper on his desk. Made from two old beer kegs and a plank of ironbark. Finding the piece of paper he is searching for he looks up.

What can a rental property command in your area over the Christmas holiday period?

2000 dollars a week sir. Depending on the house. Sometimes up to 3000 dollars a week. Or maybe more.

What phase of the moon are we currently in?

Excuse me, sir?

What is a leather jacket?

A garment, sir.

And a dog. What is a dog?

A pet, sir.

And a siren?

I'm sorry, sir?

WHAT IS A SIREN?

An electronic alarm device, your honour.

And, a mirror. What is a mirror?

Something you look into.

Do you live by the ocean Mr Knew?

Yes, sir.

How far from the ocean do you live?

Right across the road, sir.

And did you watch the telecast of the Australian Open tennis last night, Mr Knew?

Yes, sir.

And was it a clear sky or overcast while the tennis was on?

It was raining, your honour. They had to close the roof of the stadium.

Could you see the Southern Cross in your sky last night?

I'm not sure.

What is the Southern Cross, Mr Knew?

An icon sir.

How much do you charge for a haircut at your salon? I believe you cut hair for a living?

The defendant's friend looks up from his newspaper.

For you sir it would cost $65, including a shampoo and optional scalp massage.

What is a gannet, Mr Knew?

A greedy person, your honour.

I've heard enough.

The tin gavel raps. Clanging on the ironbark plank.

The Judge stands.

All rise! cries the heron. The gull-stenographer flutters.

I sentence you, the judge declares with open beak, to be taken to the shore of the great metaphor where you will be released under supervision of my feathered friends and made to skiffleboard in the tide's hem, day and night, under sun and starlight, resting only when conditions demand, until you have broken your back or some other part of your anatomy. The court is adjourned. Good Day.

Goodday me lord.

Bees

On the way back from the hills of God
The cardinal stumbled among the stones of the street
Bees were sounding a hollow in the masonry
Birds announcing the dawn with eyes closed tight
Broken filigree scattered where roadside vases once stood
A turbid Tiber, and the traffic come to a dormant shout.
He bent in amongst the pages of a book
Scouring the psalms for a reference to bees
His face drawn in shadow, his head inclined in anxiety
The scriptures drowned out by circadian agitation
Honey finally taking root among his mind's high walls.

Perec Perec

A song about Georges Perec playing Go at a café on Rue Linnè in 1974. How he loved the tricks and convolutions of the game when he wasn't looking up with a subtle grin at the street going by. Over in the Jardin des Plantes, for instance, is a mob of Australian wallabies. Bennett's wallabies, to be exact, like the ones the Napoleonic voyage saw on King Island in 1802. (The ships took a pair of King Island emus back to Paris but their descendants are not in the Jardin as the pair were the same gender. I suppose this is the kind of fact that gives Perec his hint of a grin.)

Anyway, after the game is finished he gets up and browses a bookstall. He enjoys the spines of Robbe-Grillet novels, white, with black text. When he looks up again from the books to the street everything going past is like an old memory destined for the future, as if he, Perec, is a variation of Borges' *Funes The Memorious*. With his hands in his pockets he goes back up to his apartment at No. 13 to continue writing.

Je me souviens, indeed.

He outlines the objects in the building of his memory and now the song proceeds to list these things (*Les Choses*, indeed) for you. Not for them to be reassembled like a jigsaw in your mind, nor for them to be written down again in a novel, but just for them to resonate there, as if, like the cries of the sea elephants back on the island, or a train departing from Austerlitz, they are made not of meaning but of sound.

New Shire

There's a shift in the bush
To talk of the Via Veneto
To milking buffalo
A drift away from the pokies.

There's a routine paddock
But under a quasi-Killarney sky
You know: down like a brow,
Pots of black grift in the pub.

Also anecdotes from Berlin in winter
Fill the eaves now, & the birds
Confused at the manner
Shuffle & change like the icons.

The winds are weaving
Across the stubble & houses
But the bain-marie is Mediterrasian
& the wines they're local wines.

That quasi-Killarney sky is good
For research, and roadworks.
That talk in the pub over pots
Is replacing cigarettes.

From the road the world is wide
& the cars toasty-warm inside
Outside calves & lambs are still falling
Through the dusk of a new shire.

postpastoral

grey roos on the riverflat
pale front, barky rumps
mistaken for mannagum stumps

Black Cockatoo School: *a note on novel writing*

Black Cockatoos fly over the action and reflection of a novel, lending it rhythm, stillness, timelessness, folklore, and flight. They herald its atmosphere, then govern it from the air. No matter what happens in the pages: danger, love, tears, happiness, self reflection, adventure, they are there. The earth under our feet. If the novel was a pine tree they would strip it bare; but it's not, it's a journey of the imagination and they are its consorts, its navigators and esteemed forerunners.

In adaptations that occur in accordance with the necessities of the soul, the black cockatoos appear as imagination made flesh, to quench yet another requirement of survival. So that when they call above the pages – *weeyah yeewoh* – in a voice both before and after the letters of the alphabet, that novel is given the great and immeasurable ingredient: the imaginative sky, the eternal understory, that is the signature of our life rendered anew. So that, like a Buddhist holding death at the forefront of his thoughts, this dark motif above our landscape gives birth both to the art and the life it flies through.

Visitors

cow

I travelled ocean miles in a dank ship hold for this. Was hoisted above the deck, my hooves paddling the air, and placed rudely on antipodean dock.

From there I was wattle-whipped, cursed in strine, cooped with the other tailswishing refugees, then finally delivered onto astringent southwestern grasses.

Never mind, I took to it all in good humour, cheekily even, like my ancestors in the Vedas. Before long my hide was glossy, my teats were plush, replete with pendulous drip and ooze. I found the Antarctic air-conditioning to my liking. I breathed deeply from the eucalyptus fringe.

Alas, I am a dumbfoundling cow, and resident now of a lactose-intolerant land. Brought in to feed the first Australians, I quickly learned that nobody was suckling. No-one wanted my milk!

They preferred dune currants and pigface, tangy swigs of creekwater, and yam daisy milk from the ground. They chew their own cuds and slurp on the nectary slush of local roe.

I can hear them now, dancing by a rhyming fire on the riverbank. While I stand alone in the shorn field, yearning for India.

fox

The fox came to colour the roads, to cuddle in the
cushion-bush and to sniff out sheep tongues and ears.
Then it found the blackwood lichen, the brolga eggs, the
wicked farms whereon nothing survives but hauntings.
And the fox was blamed.
For the carnage.

The darting

leaning

scampering

stretched-
out

bloodnutting fox.

While men fenced and dammed, formed their guilds,
unbridled their breeches and hung bones in monogrammed
bags behind laundry doors, the fox's cunning was redoubled.
Its tail was always disappearing around wattle-rows. And at
night, with astute eyes glinting in moonlight downwind of the
pines, the fox dreamt of a world without guns.

goat

In the mythical Land of Tragedy the goat sang the original song, a wailing form predating the Blues. Today that goat song is seldom heard, likewise the guttural carrion that for millenia fostered a union between the hard-nosed lands and the hopes of the air.

Roaming amongst bushrangers' stones the goat of the south is the hillside-cropper, the blackwood-barber, the restorer of the straight line to nature, the destroyer of the illusion of colonial freedom.

Look into those timeless eyes. See how they frame our moral universe. Observe how the desires of the goat butt against the infinite harmonies of planetary cycles.

Cock your ears amongst the Patterson's Curse. Hear the ancient song of lost illusions ring.

sparrow

Reasons to migrate:
I. *Spiritual Pilgrimage*. In a fabled 13th century career move Francis of Assisi takes the sparrow as his friend, thereby associating himself with freedom and grace. But perched on his bony shoulders the sparrow can't believe what a succour he is. Fancy, an Italian who doesn't chase birds! When the saint's mortal body finally dwindles in the airs of faith's ecstasy, the sparrow, friendless again, roams the low earth looking for someone willing to go as hungry as he.

2. *Political Exile*. Over 600 years after Saint Francis, Chairman Mao orders the People's Republic to scare sparrows off the crops. The peasants, waving dutiful sticks, make the birdhearts panic, wings go like whirligigs, those who don't fall from hunger and exhaustion hear a distant shriek: a cockatoo announcing raucous freedom in a far off land. The peasants cry as the sparrows depart, to nibble happily at cakecrumbs in the gutters of the Lifestyle Republic.

3. *A Life Of Art*. Meanwhile Mademoiselle Edith, *Lo mome Piaf*, sang from the demi-monde, with no regrets, and no superannuation plan either. She suffered as she sang, for the gaunt hearts around her, she filled their baguettes with emotionally blue cheese. When the coarse winds of man finally combined with the heart's brief tenure to bring her to ground, her song remained miraculously airborne. *Listen*…can you hear it now, flying out from that tinshed window on the seaskirts of the red centre?

sheep

The lamb of god is *baaaing* for guidance, bleating fatty acids all over the land. Guileless as weather it harries the yams, herding women and children over the clifftop.

But now watch the innocence of the sheep's own tumble. Now hear the heartbeat beneath all the wool.

For who cries when the lamb of god dies?

Not the dreamtime ochres, definitely not the longsocked shires.

Not the Greek gods either, smashing tectonic plates full of oil and rosemary. Nor the Roman's Jove or old Moses fingering his tablets in the sky.

Come on sheepy, it's time to get local. Shed the horrors of genocide, shuck all the icons, fess up to your role as a friend of the poor.

Yes, time to show us the real ewe.

carp

Ye being a common fifher with a bent for trophy and riverflefh take this Incorrigible Waterlord o the Brown Fathoms (alive if poffible), scovr him, and rvb him clean with Water and Salt, bvt scale him not, then open him, pvtting the Obdvrate Fox o the Streams, with blood and Prvffian liver (which Ye mvft saue when Ye open him, it being tangy still with Danvbian Songs) into a small pot or kettle; then take a migrant's Thyme and Eternity, of each half an auenging knvcklefvl, a sprig of Conuict Rofemary, and another of Sporting Savovry, bind them into two or three coarfe bvndles, and pvt them to the Stvbborn Aquatik Squatter, with fovr or fiue whole Onions, twenty pickled Oyfters, and three Small bvt lnfvrgent Anchouies. Then povr vpon yovr Noxiovs Ariftocrat as mvch Claret Wine as will only couer him; and seafon yovr Claret well with Exotik Cloues o Enuironmental Regvlations, and the rinds of Oranges and Lemons (or whateuer other Frvits of the Landgrab are in yovr kitchen garden), couer yovr pot and set it on a quick evcalyptvs fire, till it be boiled; then take ovt the Great Old Endvrer, this Manvfactvrer o Darknefs, Ovr Thickfkinned Sqvire o Tvrbidity, and simply lay it hvmbly with the broth into the difh, and povr vpon it a third of a povnd of *Johnny-Come-Lately*, properly gridded and beaten with a Nvtty & Paftoralifed Wrath, add half a dozen spoonfvls of Infra-red Svperiority, the yolks of two or three Brolga Eggs, with some of the Herbs and Ideas shred, garnifh yovr difh with more Federation Hypocrifies and Other Great Philofophies and so serue it vp.

cane toad

Wiki-defn / /Est. 1935 – Cane Toad, rumoured brother of a Central American plantation owner, deemed uncouth and so exiled; also forgotten cousin of a great writer, now beer-bellied scrubland entrepeneur, bastard scion come to rent a prison colony. And to remind the nation: there are no checkpoints but particles of us, there is only a tendency to *denouement*.

Psalm No. 35 / / – (Bufo *marinus*) – Vermin visitor, Gold Coast laird, faunal fascisto with landgrabs on your mind. *Have mercy* on *us*. Rapacious, unrepentant, relaxed as worshipped sun, *hear* our *prayer*. We petition you, as history's choof of train-line into healing upland moors, as our own internet creep into chthonic traditions of mother earth. Save us Almighty One, from the Punchline of Providence. *Amen*.

Note of Urgency (Classified) / / – Heed Him Ye Immortal Regulators! Sun and Moon and Wind. Ocean, Soil and the CSIRO. He wears no belt, his heart is indentured, his neo-liberal girth splays over all subtlety and astringency. He invades the strining virgin's chamber, fingers the presets of her pink smartphone, spreads the weed of credit across the naivete of the backyard.

Memo (re: Press Release) (PMO) / / –

ALL HAIL THE EMBLEM OF OUR OBESE NATION!!!

The Humble Hardworking Toad.

hare

Enchantment travels across these waters. The hare that scuttled past plush forths full of fairies now sits diamond-eyed in the astringent pub. Telling slow tales. Like the one about the dying man in the hospital bed and how his family travelled far and wide, from all points of the geologic compass, from their campsites and shacks and flats and caves and caravans scattered through the hollows and hills of Victoria, to sit with him at his passing through. And how he waited alone for them, for so long in the big country that he began to equate their arrival with the coming of his end.

Until, one deep gray afternoon, looking sag-eyed and raw-rimmed out the window into the hospital grounds, the dying man saw a scamperflash, a blazing hare going over a bean-green rise. He was immediately revived. By the time his sons and daughters, brothers and sisters, buxom old grandmothers, rubbishy aunts and ruminatory uncles, and even his great great grandfathers arrived, by car and bus and train, by foot and horse and cart across reawakened routes of sympathy, as if all rounded up by the hare, the dying man was sitting up smiling, the sports pages layed open on his pyjamas, eating cashew nuts.

camel

In the beginning the camel brought the sophistication of the apple-scented hooka to the brown riverbends. Where once the swagman and bullocky of the outback had yarned in parched cadence suddenly they were fired into song. The dervish whirled in the ironbarks. An imaginary belly danced in the billy-boiling night. Philososphic inquiries, over damper and ash, soared to the stars. Visions were decanted over squeezebox tunes, glassy mirages proclaimed.

Soon the camel was being blamed for this flowering of decadence in a droughted and termite-stippled land. High-breeched emissaries were sent out into the scrubs. Recriminations began, harsh penalties were enacted.

An Outback Inquisition was underway.

Swiftly and effectively the blaze was doused. The hooka was banned. But the camel was blamed.

The bullocky returned to his lonely old life in the long paddock.

At night he mimicked the camel by spitting with disgust into his campfire on the barren bends.

And the swagman? Well, one songless night he bellydanced into the billabong and was never seen again.

donkey

When the first Australian explorers thought of taking mules on their expeditions into the interior the mules dug their heels in, being historically indisposed to the follies of *homo sapiens*. They had thought, in the dark swill of the ship's sway, that they were coming to a new country, where they would be treated in a manner fitting their indispensable role in both books of the Bible. But no, now they were expected to carry an entire colony's scheming on their backs and go treading red dirt, hot plains and saltbush.

It was a scandal!

So the donkey was found wanting in the Southern Land, both for pliancy and an ability to traverse great distances. Once the word got out that they were strangely sensitive their jobs were given to the bullocks, and pretty soon, in this land of misunderstandings, they were being eyed off for PET FOOD.

Nowadays, if you travel far enough north, you might see the visionary anchorite-mule, Antony of Groganville, just southwest of Cooktown. Legend has it if you look into Antony of Groganville's eyes you see the Good Lord weeping, not at his burden in the garden of Gethsemane but at the disrespect his poor donkeys have put up with at the bottom of the world.

cat

The slinky fur, in a cliche of cunning, is not smart enough
to beat the poison of our town.

She threads her way through sagey olearias, finesses
around housesides, steeps her pied hind among sheoak
whispers, clubrushes of the riverflat, rusty sculpted reeds.

Her spiny tongue swipes. Anticipating proud portions.
Feathered baubles – blue wren, willie wagtail – slapped on
the masterly hearth. She may even taste the shy banquet of
the clifftop bristlebird.

Either way the extirpation is fixed. Simple. Euclidian.

Alas, dear cat. Here comes the milk of human kindness,
poured out amongst the stars. A deadly planet drops into
your bowl.

Lap lap thirsty cat.
You are the
songkiller.

For whom the bell tolls.

panther

When the phone would ring the painter would rise.

Dressing like an old sealer in his pampooties and jars he would truss his easel, suckle up pigments and bundle up brushes, set forth into the ocean of trees.

From high on a shoulder behind the town, in a blackbarked swale above a winking dam, the panther has disappeared again.

The painter arrives and peers into the scene. He sniffs the air houndishly for the image, even bending down to inspect the mythical tread in the sundew.

Accepting his fate – Panther Sighting No. 62 – he sets up to paint.

The Landscape.

What once has been and is no longer there.

Littoral

It's not love that concerns me here
(love like the bed and banks of the river)
it's the pixels in the air of creation
not the initial singularity that made them
but the bitter way they gossip and hang about
like gumleaves inciting the colony to pyromania.
It's the consequence for birds being spliced
by the commentariat's turbines, our decorous lives
like puffed-up taxidermies floating downstream
towards a billboard of the sea – yes, that's what scares me:
the way a dreamy gushing debouchment is now
just another easy way to cut & paste the land.

The Dream Down

We dreamt a census:
despite everything it is not that difficult
to live in a place with more birds than humans.
Big cities for instance, which in recent years
have been caustic with traffic
and have switched to admiring themselves
as vertical arts & garden precincts
retain, would you believe, a ratio of 1.4 avian souls
To every *homo sapien*.

Admittedly these souls are predominantly
mealy mouthed starlings and utilitarian seagulls
but nevertheless the stats remain.
If it's got wings, it's a bird.

Of course country towns which droop in the foreboding heat
of our relationship break-up with the land
abound with birds in shadows.
Bush pigeons fidgeting in eaves
budgerigars fibrillating in arboured cages
black-backed magpies yarning with bachelors
on the chartreuse skirts of the golf course.
All this, across the shires, adds up to a mean
of 3 birds for every man, woman and child
in our rural metropoli.
No matter how small, how big, or how hated or pungent,
or caged or adored, or lacking in cuteness or diseased
or tiny and drab, a bird is a bird
is a bird.

In our dreamt census however, a disturbing trend.
The bird to human ratio was slowly, but surely,
increasing in favour of the feathers.
Pretty soon, according to our shared pillow of booby-down,
birds will be back as conductors of trams
herons will help little old ladies across the road
and all complaints relating to your treatment
by Centrelink or the Banks
will be adjudicated by galahs.
Even bowling clubs in the dry-throated Mallee
will have grass parrots on the committee.

We stop sometimes, in posthuman 21st century dream-daylight,
to listen to the ever-increasing *raaark* & *wee-yah*,
the flip-flap of birdy wings about us.
When the dusk resolves into scrubland mist
or twinkling acid lights on the river
we suspect we hear nightingales.
Even well after midnight
when executives, superannuates,
                school captains and Big Issue salesmen
are sound asleep on their own dream-down
we hear not one, or three, but dozens
of owls hooting the moon.
That's about the time we usually wake up
as if to an uneasy augury.
We turn on the light
compare notes and compile stats
in the terrible silence of dawn.

Plovers

We will treble-etch *ALARM*
onto the air if you approach us
for we are with kin
on slushy ancestral ground
and when frost thaws into spring
we have young the size of dewdrops
and we protect them.
So hear our agitation
clashing amongst the bracken
in the sideways rain
and find us gawky at your peril.
We round upon intruders,
we score them with our spurs,
and in the starry night
we haunt them with a sleeptalk
riling the dark with warnings
that sound as if we can climb the sky.

Moth Symposium

It's party time: the earth here turns
under a magniloquent host
once a great valley now conducting
the dark ocean's energy from on high.
Frogs pobble in the still-moist
of late spring, school-leavers drum
& bass sincere mimicry, magpies
are compelled to ask this midnight moon:
What spirit is this which conjures
life out of the mind like dahlias
for an annual festival? And why should peace
be a thing no man has made
under stars dying while still pointing
in eight different directions?
It's true, freedom lacks explanation,
won't survive unhatched, cannot be elected.
The night unbridled pulses on
the symposium of moths on the windows
electrified by life's lack of tenure.

The Village Scale of Clear Philosophical Light

The village scale of clear philosophical light
The sunlight and wind
Characters on the bright unsealed street
Playing roles between the leafy tree canopies
Demonstrating the psyche of light & shadow, in motion
The soul visible, its tendencies
To sing (like a bird)
To take flight (like a bird)
To symbolize (like a human)
To laugh & cry (like the weather)
To remain (like the earth).
The water too: river, cistern or rain
beading the petals (look!)
dewing the petal colours (look!)
slaking the thirst (even for clichés!)
So that each day of the world is viewed afresh
Through a clear pool.
This small round stone the earth
In the middle air, the limpid pool of space.
Seen in the village scale of clear philosophical light.

Fishmonger

I am not shaggy like a sharkboat skipper
nor magnificently marked as the whale.
Myths come in plastic with longlines
of packager addresses printed
                                        and processing outfits
rather than postcodes of the deep.

And the lights! The lights!
of the refridgerated showcases at anchor there
are strong and stable. No sputtering
wick of spermaceti glow
worrying the brands or blackening
                                        the price-tickets
fluctuating the margins or furrowing the mind.

All is regulated beyond undulance of sea
                                        or phrase
our wonder weighed, parcelled out
our songs in strict quotas due to the time
when we forgot to sing.

Yet still the loyal mass of ocean surges
wheeled up from reefs on trolleys
cooked in the cauldron of dry humours.
We are surrounded by a spiny detritus
                                        of soup-stock
something you'd survive on in prison
                                        if you could afford the walls.

Scottish Shop

I don't see any battled tartans over the wet fields
But the soft cloth on your ankles, round your neck
Is a swatch of colors in the main wide street.
Scotland's in Ireland's shadow until the mountains
Argyle is confined to golf courses until the wintercoast.
There's a million heraldries to follow under the bar-heater
& boxes of pewter mugs with which to drink of your connection;
Hear the music the tinkling teaspoons make as you sort them.
Hear the pipes come over the hills of the eftpos & conversation.
It's a cloth & hued crypt this shop, a paraphrase of legend
The grades of wool a strange & muffling heaven
As clouds drift by in the southwest sky like clans.

The Environmental Flows Group Visits The Reservoir

Agenda & Discussion: whether it's possible to fother the scour-pipe
is a local debate misheard by the coots on the dam.
What they see and hear (footsteps, chat)
only makes them fibrillate and cacophonate.
The sepia sheen of our subject (ex-water catchment facility)
perforates with panicky feet & wings.
Lambent waters no longer mirror the messmate amphitheatre
ruffling instead into seams of splash, staccato strife, our best intentions
over white paper print-outs and washed-out Powerpoint
like so much sediment in the stream.

Evidence Based Outcomes: It is true that mud such as ours
kicks up an amoral fuss.
But annually at least there comes such a strong rain event
that profound volumes of this eely world are turned over naturally.
The subfusc rises, marl comes to light, the sky's reflected image
mutes to benthos.
Upstream inflow no longer pools between glasswort, heavenly inflow
taps politely no more but gatecrashes the structuralist dream.
Truth is an organic scour remaining impervious to human bullet-list
or pipe.
It is at such times that fothering becomes quite impossible.

Recommendations:

- Give yourself to the river.
- Know its lyric reed, epic pulse, its pH, potable and anoxic moods.
- Know too its fish-faces, herb flesh and gleamy dreams.
- Sing about the resettling of coots on the sheen.
- Read prints of the landrail in the glasswort fringe.

- Know the resemblance of silt to this committee.
- Know also that in the riparian world a revolution is always at hand.
- Prioritise yon balladry of watershed to estuary.
- Wait patiently for the denouement at the river's mouth.
- Listen to the nightgush of this land's sex and paradise.
- Study the spectrum of quiet towards silence.
- Celebrate the annotations of dawn: a parrwang magpie's liquid fluting, the connewarre swan honk & kookaburra song-ladder.
- Assist such underknown choirs to flourish again as family.

Photocanto

As if the coast has twisted around, *contrapasso*
from a manuscript view through the mouth of the cave
to a tourist summer full of headlights and eyes
I have reached back down to the base of the wood
screed tradition's piled-up dune, observed how
the recklessness of gods inspires developers
noted how the first lyrical habitats were deduced.

Traffic becomes the pen across the page, a metaphor
like a furphy, vowels engorged, consonants always
overtaking sugar-rich, where collision dreams an instrument.
Virgil traded in for GPS guides us to the marshes
where publishers pry into carnage as if into hard rubbish
where the clotted lure of acidic seas is a generation
surfing a wave corrugated with photographers.

A Rolling Bequest

Like the land-grab descendant who rose from his hedges
to leave a quiet 3 mil to the footy club
when no-one was expecting anything but cloudy days
the sun shone on the green clods like a refinement.

From that moment forth if you travelled there
away from town centres to the wintry square-miles
the ancient granary organed with lakes and pools
no spire, no memorial but a prehistory of purling light,

you'd receive the fecund mix: soil, rainbows,
freshly minted horizons. Players would come for cash
from Warrnambool and Ballarat, unguarded oppositions
would get a thumping and a shock:

'How can a club without a *Target*, without a *Safeway*,
a bakery, a confabulating bureaucracy
put such emphatic numbers on the board?
How can a farmscape so independent and slushy

produce a systematic game plan *as well as*
enjoying verandahed nights of frogs and stars?'
To be sure it was all most unusual,
decivilising even, as if the bequest was stained,

as if waterbirds had coached them, or the rolling stony rises
had given their fluent ball movement its architecture,
the sky its implication of dreams beyond
the dual-cabbed servos of provincial life.

Local And/Or Tourism

Some pass through gruff, others relaxed
as Fred MacMurray, but all are stretched to understand.
Living in ribbed time, fleeced and consenting
everyone keeps repeating, *click, click*,
'and how about this weather!'
Well, I am eventually spooked by it.
Poor as a mountain-snipe I fill at the servo,
lock onto the raintapped river, and humming
Panis Angelicus, like my old car's engine,
I repeat, the bowser whirring,
God forsakes no-one beside a stream.
Trouble is the banks are strewn with forgotten kites
and someone's dropped a throttle in the backwash.
I stand, still with the ghosted phrase, *click click* again,
waiting for someone from the past to adjudicate.
It's not beachhouse slides anymore it's parallel screens
And *hark*, nothing the gods ever meant to say is heard.
Bowser down it's not petrol we're pouring it's strife
as if the only thing passing us by is a tour bus.

The Memory Shell

West of the rivermouth where the convict
had lain famished after months of weird walking
I dreamt we slaughtered a kangaroo on the beach.
Butchered, it dripped thick blood on the sand.
One crimson drop struck a small shell
tossed up in a frothing moonsurf of night
and in this liquid beat a voice came to our ears.

Impossible to describe now its feeling or sound
or to configure the letters of its ancient alphabet
but just to say it sang of waves and of hills,
waves of knowledge like weather, hills of light,
also of the trees of the big ocean deep
that gives the mantling world its ancient roots.

It sang of us too, of all our affluent feasting
calling for our hearts to absorb landforms
so that blood and blood alone would not
clad the trunks and coat the leaves
tattoo the cliffs, ruin the seas and turn
the mirror-sky purple and aghast against us.

We stood, a tiny in-drawn group,
a not quite completed circle around the memory shell.
When the message it sang flew through the gap
it went out into a country of indelible memory
where we now dwell, remembering to remember.

My Kind Of Wheel

Far from the bridal rice of town
this dusk is large
as we walk on.
Time is a pump
pressure on,
the walk a valve
in the world of it all.
Give fern a chance
and she'll grow back
as amber water rivulets
along beside the flowerlets
of emblematic heath.
Across the view
in dying light
the plough has turned
the insects up
no other being leaping out
no revelation's kangaroo
just living cubits of the ground
concordant worlds, die-back & you
like stripes upon my kind of wheel
of turning crops and scrub
of dusk then wedded night.

Southsightedness

As an inventory of metaphor and allegory,
the four seasons still fail us here. This far south
we peer for tone instead of line, we note
the riverflat's bleed not the ink-strict river.
Winters for instance are not the soul-squall
the lyrics sing them as but lucid optic skins
perceiving pewter seeps and pearly spills.
Water furls through filtering banks
away from an ocean of whales northerning.
Nothing is absent: a snake memory cocked
the farmer's dam is mauve in fact
in any swale the sky might choose
night does not tranquillize but fosters
ideas in the stars: houselights switched off
the animal orchestra warrened but wide-eyed
the manuscript contents strewn outside
a still emerging day which never dies.

Lunch At Birregurra

The dual-cab lowers from the undulant districts
into the wide flat downs of southsightedness:
once a cressed valley between three tribes
then a triangulation of colonial intentions, thus forever,
at least until things are made better, a crime scene.
In the main street it's a first, or almost: we can't find a park.
Chagrined to the gutter the rain stops like us
right in the middle of Birregurra.

The pub's chilled but packed except for one vast room,
the gypsophila bistro too exy for our little tradition:
a relaxed drive over the cloudclotted ridge
away from bluewater surcharge, the way it all hinges
on memory now, the days we came over here with Dad.

But Mum's resolute so we press back out into the damp street
where I wonder aloud what the Gulidjan thought
as the clovers were hoofed the river sheepshitted up,
the yam-tonics exchanged for a liver-searing swill.

We separate: her to chew what's left of the fat
at the foodie-butcher, me peering haughtily into
plate-glass hinterlands in search of our day's salvage.

Luckily like some sad yet hick flaneur I find an empty café:
faux Alessi seats, Colac Herald benches, soups & sandwiches.
Mum finds me there and together again on contested land
we order a chalk-scrawled decoction: *Hearty Pork Soup*,
a broth at once so familiar and incongruous it seems

dished up from a lost time we never had to search for.

I tell her, slurping, that Dad would have loved it
The fat the meat the *je ne sais quoi* of filmed offal grease.
She frowns, and later on, after settling the obese bill
Declares he had a better nose for clip-joints than I do.

Grass Tree School

'It is difficult at times to repress the thought…that Tacitus was right and that peace is merely the desolation left behind after the decisive operations of a merciless power.' Seamus Heaney

My whole heartland is an auditorium
gone ghostly quiet & still –
It's strange having to talk with the grass-trees
but there are no tourist guides of this coast's genocides,
so as documents stand the hillside's shimmering fronds.
My eyes can see the song, the vestigial smiles and laughter
in the living tracery of winter sunshine,
the sheer rip of light that bounces off speartips,
but the ears do the sad understanding –
Like Odysseus at a feast without instruments
there is something inexplicable in it all,
as if the lover of a singer has had her tongue cut out –
We try politics, print and our musak of naming
but this grass tree school is already teaching
in a wide acoustic classroom every day.

Gloss

A tourist town can be nice you know
In bracing forest air
The trees like sculpted wire-work
And logfires earthing the bar.

Around 3.30 or 4.00 is best:
Clusters of green school uniforms gather
With gall and pimply shyness exempting
The perfect paving from seeming a total fraud.

Even the gloss and plate-glass shine,
Even period lettering and striped confectionery
Can recede like local gemstones at dusk
Simply by conversing with a local artist.

It is sweet then to wander under verandahs
Where moonlighters toasted shipwrecks on rocks
To relax in the craft of gypsophila & argyles
To hum in your head a reworkable tune.

Parrwang

Violins block the magpies
I poke my head around the sound
I see a wig on the ground, a stick
They used to hit you with
I call out then listen
For the echo of that violence
Of that arrogance
It bounces back neverending
Off red escarpment walls.

I stand up in the canyon of tears
Blood so deep you couldn't mine it
I whisper to my own boys
The river was sweet
But now it's full of shit and horsehair
If you don't expect otherwise
The magpie's dream is over
You've got to see the dark boys
To see the stars.

Long Prelude, King Island

In a heightened song beyond voice
the burr doesn't birl here, the grass waves
to water and we are watchers, listeners
too new on the island to mint a translation
unable to pull down lightning's metaphor
without thinking or connecting
the weather to the bluff features of man.

We walk like secretaries to place
not ploughmen or emblem
we dream at night of pale screens
beneath a pitter-patter of ideas on the roof
shuffling & shifting rather than sheafing
and rustling not whoofing & whacking
through the blowhole of the ancestors.

The tide is in every vacant page of sky
every stillness which the long prelude floods
and we are drawn to this gustwracked isle
for cloud-drama, the constant tilting march
through gales to headlands where we may see
above the loud meteorological clashing
a destiny writing itself before our eyes.

Cairn 1803

The weather approaches a salty text
written on sky and tussock fleck
wisdoms & cautions combing the hides
of wallabies, cattle, the paperbark
in steeped swamps, flayed and frogsung,
represented as tea-furlings, bark spouts
retinting the sea from every falling furrow.

Across the written white-swiped water
gannets tilt the terns' black caps
dip and rend the crestings, dancing
in the eye of one who stands bound
in boots by the cairn announcing
humanity's memorial cargo. It reads:

'We can never be at one like bird to sea
like wind to grass or cray to reef
we are forever writing but Fate composed
of the Roaring Latitudes is a knowledge
seldom surrendered to our ink-pen.'

Fighting The Seasons

When he was left behind, a farmer excused
from the faraway war, it was the aftermath
of the ghosted glens that first went into him.
Creeks breed reflections, paddocks a frame,
the sky a haunting that can't be contained.
That eagle there, for instance, the way it owned
an immense picture of the farm, knowing why
the sun and rain were arhythmic and unforeseen
their no-showings and comings-on the opposite
of church times, grainy radio, or the rates.
Something got into his brain during those years
and like leaves in a tousling wind he kept
switching ever after, between the dark pool
where all mysteries reflected close
and the hard bright land of topsoil, milk price,
the weather like grass in the bite of his working day mind.

But nothing can be buried, not forever.
The war's loneliness taught him this
the clouded hill-lines of his own internal siege
the voices threshing in his ear, creeks no longer there
where ancient fissures of the pool appear, the risk
of diving so deep to understand everything.

When the battles were over and the blokes returned
so did darkness, nor could it be explained
the perceptions of that vantaged eagle,
not something on an epaulette but high
above the tribal fights, the mothballing

of uniforms, the folding-away of medals
the knowledge too immense to enter language.

He kept thinking of that day when he was a child,
when the kind old man came, the buried souls
he pointed out, the deep pools of eyes like galaxies,
til gradually at his feet or on tractored days
it all began to reappear, beneath his plough,
stone visions left in the land's great store:
basalt flints & grinding rocks, old tools
fashioning milky ways of perpetual wonder.

He was a dairy farmer after all. And later,
when shire services curdled, they came
with a name for him – *bi-polar*:
that switching of the leaves in clouting light,
that constant return to the glint
of the pool's dark sorrow.

Gentrification

Bored with gentrification, whether it be hassling it or
my own participation
I wander off into the trees in search of other oils.
That could be the two inches of eucalyptus fuel on the forest floor
Which soothes my limbs before they catch fire
Or the tea-tree in the dunes where the fox dens are.

Those foxes sleep in the hummock during the day
(and this is where a metaphor should be inserted to carry the poem)
so as to cross the Ocean Road at night and frisk the town.
A perfect set-up: your patterned structures must go deep
into the ground
All windy gaps or rough triangles need to be stoppered
(and here's where we hear the cordless drill, the soundtrack to what
was formerly the soundtrack of the waves) otherwise the fox
will come
like an offshore investor through the rooftops of its own
uncalendared Xmas.

Why is it though (I ask) that I have such a need to wander unmetered in
those trees?
Is it the freedom all humans seek, the freedom to go and then
return, ventilated, with new eyes?
Or do I just get sick of the contagion of *Via Negativa*?
My mind, longing to bleat and carp but my soul
really needs the broader influence of aromatic canopies
(the way they glint and fall like the waves).
Otherwise these selling units aren't units they're just cages
And who could possibly live happily in a cage?

Better then (and this is where you think about the price)
to admit our own likeness to den-architecture
The sandy lintel, the loamy sanctum, where wild things rest well
Between starry raids on a plump and peacetime town.

Late Sonnet

An outcrop of summer in late late autumn
a subset parenthesised as weather in a zoo
a tor of high pressure alarming the sinuses
as lifestyle evangelists shuck off their wetsuits
what of the honeyeaters in the viscous pond
frisking blacks and yellows for dear life
chirping among families without futures or billabongs
the burning swell peels over igneous mid-tides
broiled garfish drift like pixels in the footage
so proven neurotics note strange insects
joining the lab dots between this and that latitude
the knowledge we eat seasons a spoil of victory
it's bad news for winter when scrolling distractedly
the surfwear and marchflies seem destined to kill.

Restoring An Ancient Metaphor To My Dreams

Restoring an ancient metaphor to my dreams
I travelled far and wide for the heritage breeds
not knowing exactly what I was doing
but sensing we needed something more wholesome
than anything genetic engineering can provide.
On returning home I felt the link over several days
between the making of a poem
and the construction of a building
in this case a chookhouse, strung and patterned
in recognition of the nightly fox of truth
who lives unbound from children's picture books
in a warm poem-den of its own making
in the dune hummock south of town.

This chookhouse-and-run was to be the new home
Of two hens from Barongarook, two from Winchelsea,
And two from Geelong. As they settled in
we watched a pecking order revive
from where it had languished in euphemism.
We saw how it was the opposite of that,
how it hurt, and therefore held true meaning.

For months then we were dreaming of the omelettes to come,
the frittatas and the yolk-dipped soldiers of toast.
But winter's heathlit chill had descended upon us
The sun tickling the hill-lines –
it slung its ammunition low across the sky.
In an otherwise hushed darkness we rose
with the magpie every morning
to find six hens still sleeping in their hay.

Then, nearing the end of the local footy season
the light began to come back and lengthen the day.
Our old dog still slept but the hens grew hungry earlier now.
They gathered at dawn's door like supporters clamouring
for finals tickets.
Even the new buds on the nearby peach tree
seemed to be barracking for the eggs.
The game was on. The hens preened and shone,
hassled us for grain, they clawed the ground for insects,
slurped up their rainwater, and sat blinking
in the warming gold of the wattle-spring
which brewed in the canopy over their run.
Even the old man eucalypt seemed to be asking us
to set the festive billy on the fire of fun.
The song of warmer nights felt as close now
as the sound of the sea.

And yet they did not lay.
We held discussions with sardonic farmer-friends,
feeling about as green as our slushy riverflat
though nowhere near as resplendent.
We began to suspect that yes, we'd been too puritanical
in rejecting the ecumenical acronym of ISA Browns.
Cheeky uncles licked their lips too
at the prospect of a locavore poultry banquet,
necked chooks coming their way at Christmas time.
It got to the stage that I'd almost forgotten
what we were hoping for,
our heritage breeds had become not so much pets
as the cluck-clucking soundtrack of a lack of inspiration.

Then one morning, as I went out to vinegar their water
a clean and curving arc of shell beamed up at me:
the sunlit face of a new planet in the leaf litter.
In the following days we took our turns
to taste the nectar of daily heart-rich yolk.
To me it tasted something like the faith we should always keep
in even the most ephemeral of creeks.
One night too, during that first euphoric week
I dreamt I went fox-like in the leafy moonlit run.
All around me a soft lunar light fell
on precisely what is symbolised by the sun: eggs.
Eggs in all kinds of shapes, colours and sizes.
Each shell was a house for a new world, a new universe,
Each universe had a different beginning, some rich,
some outrageously so, and every one a sort of poem.

I woke from the dream knowing that something very old
had hatched within me: an ancient consciousness in fact
of visions appearing, apparitions of natural wealth,
such simple yet nourishing things.
Human beings had been dreaming this since the world began.
In my veins I felt the old dry creekbeds running,
returning to full spate, and somewhere
in the nearly forgotten and outermost parts of my being
stars swirled through a night-sky shaped in the perfected
yet slightly unlikely form of an egg.

Eternal Slanders

currawong perched on a bulb of outboard motor
bits of fox strewn over the highway
magpies squished against black road
song-dead
pictures on the inner wall
of banksias tired and weak
kids left with a brittled legacy
a beauty crunched
a snatched-away gift at an internal party

eternal wake, eternal slanders
houses potted like stalks
disco architecture, obese rooves
a riot of vain design
on a land too dry to fashion;
this garish theft will wear back
like drift on wood
the beak of truth in the bitumen splatter
the right dosage of nectar
pumping into the clifftop leaf

A Smile At Arms Length:
Digital Emissions & Selfie Obsessions in the Landscape

1. Self Portrait In An Australian Convex Mirror

First things first – I get convex confused
with the amniotic grotto, the cave
of my ancestors who beat the mean storm
of English oppression with wintry
chagrin, alcohol, and a leaving ship.
So why should I jut out so clearly given
I strain their genes through watered-down paint
holding their courage to vanity's ransom?
No, I'd rather recede like a wave
or the wan Irish beach as they pulled away
lachrymose, unphotographed, for oblivion.
They sailed without risk assessment or passport
yet here I look blankly into the glass
as if it was my idea all along.
Wrong again, any hour I have to gaze
at me-watching-me is predicated
on the whale fluke of that lucid voyage.
Not to mention the country bashed on arrival.
A flick of the tail, a slip of the tongue
and all this would be undone, no antipode
would excuse my lack of ballast no fee
could dowry this chronic lack of something
dramatic, transoptic, in my soul
which, as you see, no family tree can shelter.

2. Psalter

Each original premise filleted for click-bait
seeking approval of noughts & ones
which jump the shark
in less time than it takes a phrase
to become an acronym, he shrugs off
the temptation to market
adds yet another analogy, spits by way
of punctuation, becomes a fish again.

Like Sweeney hurling the holy psalter
into the bottomless lake, he has thrown
the phone. Aah, what a relief.
No more subscribing to terms of privacy
he feels his gills dilating, no longer high & dry
with thumb-dancing Boeotians by the pool,
he is a-swim, the light of the world
re-registering him, scale by scale.

3. *raark, tweet, cuckoo*

The birds check their sounds against escarpments
our friend stares into the screen at his reflection
the earth surrounding splinters into laughter:
laughing shards, laughing arrows, tormenting branches
overhanging silent rocks. Green drapery on mute
sensibilities not so much aghast as mineral, without irony.
Sound familiar? This is where Face meets Geology
the slowest download of them all, fracking the mythic pool.
Cockatoos, honeyeaters, shrikes, all dwell nearby and search
not for love but for sweet Echo, *raark*, printed on air,
who with hair up or out, *tweet*, dyed or down
like the mirror, *cuckoo*, has no control over her image at all.

4. Dis-*tract*

He was texting a speech in Syntagma Square
on the black dais near where the suicides hung
wondering what's for dinner, and what Diogenes
would heckle from his barrel on the fringe.
Yet now is not *pure then* (BC) and when he began
to stride the stage, a thinker with dancing thumbs,
the memory of last night's comely Skype chimed
with an email alerting him to how he is liked
in Slovenia, Connemara, Nebraska, Canberra,
Manchester, New Haven, Bogota, Arcachon,
Kucing, Kerala, Casablanca, Alexandria,
Catania, Crow's Nest, and so on and on....
until by the time he reached the end of this elevation
he simply stepped off the stage into air.
Distraction cannot fly and finds this out
in understaffed emergency wards where fair Excel
chronicles the new disease: digital accidents
shot across the curated bow of the species
head-ons, a renaissance of RSI, screenaholic
operating systems bleeding for another wild name
or better: some de-extincted pigeon perhaps
location services disabled, furry chicks also
checking their updates, launching into air which
once a Cynic's invective painted black where
once a burning rope would have saved them.

5. Narcissus, a selfie

Googling himself the grandson of the ocean
came up with results both erotic
and disturbing. Like Time in the river Kephisos
that moves both sweet and bilious, swift
yet still, his doubling had begun.
There was something hypnotic about the river
it's ancient volume invisible
it's inner workings a silent mystery
yet it shone like a screen.
Forever famous between those banks
the body behind him, the landscape
seemed leaden, old fashioned.
Scrolling from site to site along the bank
it was always the same: his glassy face
a spring-furnished eidolon made real
an image replenished by the river
yet destined for erasure in the sea.
How though does one dive into 2 dimensions?
The surface too easy to break, the perspex
would shatter as if gunshot, the deep
undermurk would be olive-brown.
Yet this was his pining's rendezvous
the DNA of all those URLs
his auto-stalking and multi-blah.
How then to discover again the wetness
of the Kephisos flowing past?
How to swim, with someone else, forget the self
become his red salt blood?
He closes his eyes
and with his image gone

tries to contemplate the soul's disguise.
He looks into the sky
but sees the river there
a reflection of his godlike eye.
So, through the prisms of time
comes the hiss of a reversing tide.
The banks are exposed and dry
the river an ever thinning line
between screen-love and its echo.

6. Arm's Length

Only the victims seem quite real in Aleppo
or the real's opposite, which is all there is.
It's the irony of imagery, or so they claim
but hang on, they don't have claims at all
they're cold as phone-casing, confronting
as offline lovers. I have my likes
but none so preponderant or invested
as my smile at arm's length. Like my Instagram
and you like all of me, and so do I
unless those historical searchlights come on.
That's when I scroll past self-approval, turn back,
my shadow a dividend always shrinking,
until it's just me, alone, uploading

7. The Burr

'Self, that burr which will stick to one. I can't get it off yet.'
Percy Bysse Shelley, in a letter to Leigh Hunt. 1819

Self is a habit which turns
bad in a selfie. Fun is terminal
when one contracts selfie-elbow.
Self-portraiture becomes the sky
at the trillionth duplication.
We have a population problem.
The previously transparent air
is stuffed with kooky faces.
Is this an emissions issue?
Nature is all horizon.
The distant self, the wider you.
Counterfeits are never soluble.
Plastics in the sea, and all that.
Hot air conflating into solids.
We'd walk through brick walls
to find some peace, we'd die
to be left alone, yet that film
would be scary.
We've lost the remote.

Catch your breath, no, exhale.
Find your phone, no, disable
that setting. Flick the burr
when mystery is in exile
when choirs of hell
become your ringtone.

8. Boeotian

What if the camera had vision, vision and rhythm
So that when it saw me there grinning, pale arm extended
It saw an ash-grey shark savaging a surfer

What if the Dutchman's paints weren't quarried mud of the lowlands
What if they held the whole earth's roaring poem, raging truth
The elegant interiors alive with oxen

What if the mirror was not made of sand, of desertification
But held the source of all blue waves in its frame
So that we would fall and keen

What if the brown billabong did not yield the tree's brocade
So that when we leant over it, a mad Boeotian staring
Would be forever remembered and confessed to the sky

What if I looked up and saw myself in your eyes across the water
Wanting the same thing, inheriting the same anxiety
What if you could see me too, beginning to undress

9. Barometer

Higher wider deeper mirror
sailing past erupting roar
it will pass it will pass
says the captain of my heart
tapping to find real pleasure
on the glass. Ruskin put clouds
in bottles, science monitors
evangelical dials yet
the biospheric you & me
wear clothes. Cumulus passes
quicker than fashion yet
is more permanent.
Sky is temperament, gentle
sunshine the moral guide.
The sound of trees for instance
our climbing for birds' nests
smashing eggshells on the ground
of impulse-storms.
Zeus had it right – we
swallow the world, alpine perspectives
pedal this digestive view, spring
of our appetites, autumn of retrospect.
It has been a harsh winter
in ignorance of this. Manufacturing
is symptomatic in the west. Trust
the fault-line to shudder like that
Lest we forget *les temps*
time is weather, its steady-state
our finest highest truest shrink.

10. Humboldt Embosses a Monkey

White as an alp is the page where I write
something of the orange-tipped mask of light
clambering out of me, a body from its clothes
a line unfurling, the scent from a rose.

The point is sharp, it spears into gaps
between creatures and their names, truth and 'the facts'.
'Herr Prussia where did you say your instinct got lost?'
'Oh, somewhere in that moment between the *em* and the *boss*'.

So the concert needs a singer, we have to score the lines
same as any agriculture growing rusted in the tines
first the brow, then the teeth, a light covering of hair
from Cartagena to Vienna all's connected there

like conscious pain & the cosmos, the chatter in the trees
in approval of the pencil breaking Europe at the knees
till it's begging, even squealing, for my wisdom of the day
'Let the monkey be your mirror, anytime you lose your way'.

The Habitat at Christmas

This fire a far-right riot of forest-infused violence
made painterly by the jib of phone screens.
What inflames such vistas on a cloudclotted ridge?
Try millennia of outlawed mythologies surrounded
on three sides by alchemical farming then trumped
by the invasion of Bing Crosby's Christmas at L.A. levels.
Brands now universal as the transmission of burning bush
go red raw in an overpopulation of eucalypts
and what genius can franchise an evacuated coast
selling perfect tubes with no *visible achievement* inside them
a brochure of freedom beneath particulates glowing
the plume's convected ear-trumpet moaning while quolls
chainstoke through a marshall-stack, habitat flaring,
the red-orange tide a last resort from summer's tourist rip.
For days the smoke replaces mist, a holiday fuse brooding
before the media I receive a cartoon depicting
the holy couple on the wrong side of a refugee fence
the Christmas star on the other side. I rub smoke
into the scene until all pathos is obscured except for
the sound of the Christ child coughing himself hoarse.
On Soundcloud someone asks whether that's a barking owl
I've sampled, rare enough in these parts, plonked on top
of that bed of Juno. Well, there's no point laughing
about nature illiteracy now, and anyway,
laughing through a fire mask is hardly music.
On the cooler Monday we walk in temperate interludes
with light like goat's milk strewn along the bush track
every leaf's a curling match, every thrush a prank caller,
an anonymous personage lost on history's breeze.
A wedge of sea is paint through the branches, a chopper

like a whitecap droning there, the plume retracted
yet the wisps warning of the warming new years to come.
I caught the news driving into Geelong and then released it
like a Cape Otway koala back into the wild. Later I was told
across the extended family that they were coaxing visitors
to come and burn. It used to be trampolines, ice cream cones,
surfmats & coconut oil suntans, now it's a moral duty
to small tourism businesses susceptible to financial anxiety.
Well, smoke seeds its own biome, fire hatches and tires, incarcerates
and incinerates desire. The cricket plays on however,
in creams and painted green, a test indeed, not of character
but of market forces. And so the Great O is choking
with agnostics not used to conflagration, not like Andy, Roy, and the
rest of the Wye CFA, whose humour is as dry as the conditions.

The Meaning Of The Parish Names

paraparap & angahook,
gnarwarre & modewarre,
barrabool & boonah,
jan juc & duneed.....
was it red iron bark
or a spanish word,
a place where you can glimpse the sea,
was it a scottish word,
a kangaroo doe?
of no known aboriginal connection?
was it musk duck,
a moodi-warr,
a sandy sandy,
or a rounded mountain
place of ironbarks,
was it a *place* at all?

i deny any connection whatsoever your honour
to the parishes mentioned i don't know god nor
have i met him i know the places where i live
and work your honour not these religious pasts,
men i'd say but with the worth of ghosts
no congregation have i worshipped with your honour
i am proud to be free and unacquainted
with a parish at all, i like my life
and resent any reference to lard or waistcoats,
that was all my ancestor's thing but me,
am i free to go?

were they Spanish eyes

or English belly-rolls,
shepherd's pie,
he'd have to eat it on his own
wouldn't he? Just him
and wind in iron sheets
was it the kind of stone
you could fashion,
and was the parson Californian,
there were long prayers said
at the first land sale,
four blocks selected,
afterwards there was a stew,
was it bare on top
that hill was it heath,
did you spell the name
ng
did you spell at all,
were they country sections,
square miles,
a chain
or tithe,
or land nearby a church?
who baled the hay,
mended the sacking
did you?
has the price upset the ground
the seed
the bu
the barrabin
the djirrm

do you tend those eastern lots,
was it rounded
and bare
the hill?

the hill to me is rent your honour my sun
comes up on lists you see i earn no interest
on original things, some say there was a well,
a spring some say there was a god
but when we made our search we met
with sand, & three old bottles of 1865,
but empty you see, empty, so no
i see cockatoos rise over trees,
my flowering gums, or should i say
my wife's but god do i have to explain
the archives of my land i was of the belief
that it was mine, excepting for the chain
of riverbank where tourists fish,
on my world's edge, in its midst but
what is that to me, to give is to receive,
the rent i make helps to keep me well...
no effort on anyone's behalf
can prise from me what i do not have;
take my surfboard take my car
i will see the police but you
cannot steal from me something
that i do not have your honour,
something that i do not have
i repeat, you cannot steal
from me something
that i do not have

III

Know A River

Know a river
any river
but know a river.
Know that life passes
at the river's pace
that staunch limbs
get snagged till they twist
and easy lissome fronds
go floating seaward.

Know a river's justice.
Know that borders never last
that energy laps and erodes
kisses and flows,
that even dry banks
try to tumble towards god.

Know that it takes
all sorts to make a river:
busy insects, gawky birds,
cluey fish & deeply migratory dust,
parsimonious eels, old-man traps,
sky-mirror and rippling wake,
just as the winter-into-spring
often turns a river to a lake.

Know photos of a river
know sedge
know it in a boat
know its scent from some way off.

Know that life's tempo
scythes through moments
of hot and cold
that deepest down is coolest
that shiny rivertops perform
the magic tricks of this world.

Know what it is
to sit & cry into a river
adding *yours* to *its*
as water draws grief
like a bucket at a well.
Know its wild boyhood too
its jetty planks when baking hot
and cypress cubbys
where your desire caught fire
where it flows and cascades.

The river knows
nothing lasts forever
forever passes like the weather
things flash on the scales of skin
and seep houseward.
All longing is natural.
Remember as a kid
the affinities you felt
with tea-coloured streams
and glittering reaches
how a river was your sister
the perfect listener,

and make it so once more
to solve the drought in loneliness.

Go about life
with the river
and its sibilant whisper
so that moments
hours & days
can sow your moody spirit-fields
with tides and currents
with winds that go on showing you
the ephemera of knowing.

The Cirrus Tree

He walked
in a ziggurat of flies
after screening billy tea

Black, sage-green and white
the colour of teatree flowering
along the track

Crunch, crunch, tap, tap
go his feet, his staff
in the dirt of the bush red road

Plenty have left him
he is not lost, the flies' music
will leave him too one day

In that place
there will be no leaves in the tea
the birds will come to have their share

In that place
the wind gets up
a gliding high in the cirrus tree

Stars dance
where he dreams under wattles
of light turning into sound.

He walks on
toward the pound of horizon
where the work gets done

the timber cut, the lathe revolved
around the jargon spiel
of top cockies

He takes his time
where gumleaves shine
along the line of a new morning.

Animals Forever!

We counteract the traffic with music on CD
and the tiny buzz of wrens and such are sacrificed
to the battle. The leaves of the cabbages wilt
as much from drumbeats as from trucks
and no amount of fey cello will ever please a galah.
The wattlebird when it comes will not have come in from the bush
but from the garden, as first concieved in the Book of Genesis
by some brilliant guy, who after years of implacable light
in the desert, finally got himself a study to work in.
Like him we'll sit amidst our precious things,
with little windows administering doses of light,
with paintings by meretricious people on the walls
and books by people we'd be nervous to meet,
and we'll encode a distant memory, of things like the sky
and bees and worms, and lizards at the fingertips.

If we go far enough we may remember caterpillars
in the same way we'd remember fashions from the 80's,
we'll recall cocoons even, and the memorial delight of finding them.
Yes we were tourists even then, as holiday children,
roaming the trees for stinkbombs and bluetongues
like the cars round here comb the road in search of coffee.
And if our studies are particularly quiet
like the man from the desert we'll go deep
and rediscover the grunt we made when we crushed the cocoons
with the rocks we'd scratched up by the creek.
That'll bring a jolt to the quiet study, a violence like the Old
Testament itself,
but a gang-gang creaking at a safe distance outside
will make us smile again and decree to ourselves that children

are wilful & insensitive, obstreporous & murderous,
until they learn to behave as you must to live a harmonious life.

So in between the melodies and the wheels our lives click on
stepping on bare ground two or three times a year
climbing a tree maybe once a decade
having a good cry sometime soon that never comes
inverting our tantrums all the way to the cemetery.

Only there, at the odd funeral, will the birds & the worms,
the sky and the bees win out again.
Huddled in the sun, with the celebrant parroting
the CDs left back in the parlour, the cars quiet & ashamed
in the carpark,
we'll watch the bee buzzing round and wish it would sting.
We'll catch a gleam of the light on the moist skin of a worm
revealed now in the clods of the dug grave beside,
and wish it a safe journey back out of our sight.
Then looking up with a sigh we'll notice the sky
how many possibilities it has when compared to a ceiling.
The clouds could well be the faces of the dead,
the blue around could be their happiness being freed
and we'll remember again an oath we made
as children: "To live outside with the animals forever".
A spoken oath, a group of words never written,
except in the precious script of dreams
which we'll then realise we've forgotten.

Sum of Creation

Am I the young Victorian in the sepia overcoat
All green countryside versus factory belch, melancholy
At the lack of a military threat, made dowdy
Then brilliantly drunk by a friend off the boat
Whose inheritance of sonorous utopias allows him to see
My dreary literary walking as time in a sod-rich key?

And yet I continue to narrate, my nib scratching for the sake
Of the daily egg & spud, my wife maturing from the inside
Her porcelain delicacies expanding to a folksy beauty
So loving as I walk, *a stór*, reflective too as love's swan lake
Her windscuffed watertop a dynamic local lens
Something still alive, worth living with, as opposed to a drying fen.

I give and take what I can then, over-stimulated, porous
And like Hopkins on his unpublished clifftop am revived
As if the actual world of sky and heath is liturgy
Patterned and painted for an ultimate target audience
The sum of creation not quite adding up to a basic wage
Yet spilling over with tears, and words on the page.

Though the world's constantly in cataract we find freedom
in a single bead, and sounds come gushing out of us.
This is the music that soars with trees and burrows underground.
So that's me in gloaming mode, borrowing a poet's spare dusk
Drinking gallons of water as I climb the night mountain
Hoping that tomorrow I'll come rushing back down as the river.

Connewarresong

Your swan eel-neck a periscope
above greenskirt nest the lake
fibrillates with pleasure & wings
a honk in rustling reed
the ridge of gumclad stone
echoes into seeping dark
the bark falling cursive
on the moon-risen track.
Roo claws notate codes in clay
the pianola of a small bird's wings
chirping past
uses wind
breeze
luff
breath of life.
I climb through leaves
on rose-gold feet
to the subfusc of watery dreams.
I cooee across hill-lines
sounding heaven's amplitude
while at my feet ant-nest organ pipes
transport the music home.

In Colac

He took a heavy load from Murray St to the shore
of the lake. Made of blood and wood he hauled it
across shaved grass of congruous blocks till he saw
the saltscript on which it lay heaped, the punctuation
of succulents. Time scrawled on rocks by children.
Wisdom pouring out of district burden.
In wide light he weighed it all to understand
what was washed up by gun and sheep:
umbrage in the churches, sorrow in teacups, lace curtains
wistful in the breeze now corrugating the lake.
Balance became a spray of rosellas blocking the sun.
Music the farmwork of a distant country. He felt for
what could be done in such ancestries of light
with darkness made of words and their shadows
lines written under the tongues of the shore.

The Old Dream Resurfaces

I get into a pleasant email loop
with four old male friends about times we spent
in scrubland pubs on parched lake beds of dust
where we smoked and wrote and gazed out windows
or peered through verandah shade at long skies
driving round bends just as long and slow
as a smalltown dog or a hard won punchline
it took us years to understand.

It seems it took us years to understand
a helluva lot – the endless drought
that pushed houseprices down like a bore.
Speaking of which, it's a curious reprise
to think of escaping out there, cheap seats
are usually cheap for a reason.
Not that we've got much choice being poets
though a road trip is imaginable:

five of us in bohemia's sedan of schemes
chatting by email about the images
you won't see on a postcard yet you wish
still for correspondence of that nature
memories overlapping like the seasons
clouds clearing in the cerulean glare of a big past
a big doctor's house and redgums with sheep
the lake where love turned sour but camping's still cheap.

Water's a huge problem these days unlike
any other yet somehow still the same
perhaps if we just chatted all day and night
recumbent in middle age but poets, yes,

seeking solutions in each other's hearts
rather than out beneath those brutal skies
where any unsuspecting reptile can
be pulverised by road-train tyres

we'd be better off. Speaking of which
how are you feeling, what are you feeling
about the night we laughed and sang
when time was music waking up the street
which won tidy town 3 years on the trot
because there was no-one to mess it up
all of them gone to the city as if to war
and us, as usual, driving the other way.

I see it clear, getting up after lunch
with a penchant for old timer threads,
racing suits and well made shirts, waistcoats too
they saw us coming and wondered politely
why we weren't working or where we were heading
or whose sheep we weren't shearing but writing
was never mentioned till we got upstairs
after stumps and became our own juke box

blasting dreams from the open windows
of poets and dreamers who were our heroes
not misshapen veterans or shiny racehorses
but eloquence and euphony and wit
lucidity that needed to be read twice
or every night like the constellations
the stars and planets of the mind's page
the pattern of that unwitting reptile.

Euclid's Sea Eagles

Through a sea-lens of light
		on the east coast of time
between the *tsss* and *whoof*
		of the flood tide blowhole
and the silent recumbence
		of Sea Elephant island,
three sea eagles isocelize,
		equalaterise in an html sky.
Banking turbine high
		uploading columns of air
they form a tryptich stylus
		in rhyme-relation
to the alternatives of a square.
		While we shellgaze in curios
of kelp and brine as if searching
		for solutions to sustain us
through the day they climb
		steep then indisputably
down to spec on dune-tombed limbs
		installed as if by Euclid's whim
between theories of desire
		and the mullet-gorged stream.

Double Rainbow

The wind beats and harries
slanty rain etching trees, danking webs
that drape charred trunks
making a gauze of the hills.

Spirits scatter in the air
and a sound is attached
like a spook in an abandoned house
the ticking inherent in a flue.

When sound's wild breath drops down
birds tweet again in the interstice.
A currawong signals flight over a paddock
roofing-tin becomes the twang of departure.

Thus our lives soak in, are rebuffed again
our eyes in a storm of paint, our ego a gale
all our effects like pixels over the hills
carried away by appetites of air.

Time shares its lair with nature
its roaring, its lilt, its bluff.
Each end we endure gives rise to a new exhalation
each death a double rainbow with magpies.

Song-way

The river tells me you're all still here
As I hear the water break sluicily
The echoes moving slowly towards me
Then away, rebounding off the bank
Where I sit at the foot of my dear contemporary
The river-rope mannagum.

The water's become moving skin again
Skin with the sky in it, the boobiallas,
I hear the return, the whole riverflat a body
With temperaments and inclinations, quail, bursaria,
It takes a bit of getting to know.

Once it's family though it can't be forgotten
Nor too what you've had to endure
All the way out to the seven sisters
In the process of us coming to be here.

It's ironic how you remind me of the practicality of hospitality
The way you've returned to tell us you never went away.
But deeper than that you remind me of the river's flow
Going past pain going past pleasure
Taking logic from the cosmos and not from the script
And whisper-listening all along of course
All along this song-way to the sea.

still dying

Recollections are like dairy boats
 punting through cormorant-maps,
through silken black water as screws tighten
 & gusts of nail-guns bring shelter
from time, shelter from ambling,
blood flows flatstick through veins,
dreams turn into mere realities,
 wrens & finches mop the exposure
of slaters & fat worms turned over,
bright exposure, and in the loft
 a thought runs to the thin edge of its wedge.

Above the batons & tin, above the thought
 the stars of live time shine,
joints in god's frame, old miracles still dying,
 still shining on our plague coalescing,
shunting, snipping the tune-strings,
 still ringing some bell way out there

Constant

is the wind, the strait a-roar
days, nights, the face of the moon
a voice of the sun, telling stories
from the back row, the spotlit core.
Performer and audience (in one)
preferring text to gloss (I listen)
an egret watching estuary sheen
for fry that will sustain us.

See it in luminous network of night sky
the storied hour, guide, lore,
old timers mirrored in high heavenly joints
toasting us, showing us (if we'll agree)
the earth turning in the lock of space
to find your keys you've got to lose them.

Things are large, small, purple, voluminous, not easy to miss:
the obfusc of electrical light
cotton wool in mussel ears
how we mishear the original engine
see jocular sprites in branches of the heaven-tree.

'Vast, vast, a-vast' sing O little thee
fishing there in the lost notations
of what was, what is now, and what will be.

Frankincense

We take a loft from the haystack
and re-fume the barn.

We lie in a structure of past sacrifice,
of austerity, of work, of functionality.

We want to forget pictures and styles
and try to be vegetable.

We drive utes & troop-carriers
to arris great distances.

The cadence of beeps is in our loft,
the red meters.

The wind is Shetland,
the crostoli are munched on.

Our town is working its jaw
for the resurrection of the lost word 'village'.

Our dreams are of muses
that are much harder won.

Deambulation – a Sonnet

Before you decide that the word *deambulation* is too difficult
Remember that ceasing to walk is the coagulation of habitudes.
Feel your notions pickle as your limbs thicken your mirror bloats
And old dust refuses to declare undying love for you. A film settles
over your heart, your legs seem made as if to hang from your hips
like two dead bushrangers the authorities have brought back to town.
They dangle, adventures sprung, as if only for photographers.
Thus the undulance of *deambulation* is worth not rearing from.
Though simple is good, unwalked is binary. As in doofdoof, or *clunk*.
Noli timere, the dying poet texts to his love, to enjoy the word
is to ambulate itself. Death shall be as moving as what happens next,
which twig will crack which bird will shrike which song will come to mind.
And so, to desummarise: unfix your capacity. Allow yon syllable sounds,
the copious life-language where old opposites unify, to walk in you.

Gain A Reedy Companion

The swagman is drifting beyond the boundary road
with every mile an old name falls from him like bark.
In the gloaming he stills, questions whether the
billabong is drinkable,
worries again why the owls are low-noting so.

It's surprising only one hour's tread from town,
already hellraisers have been displaced
by the heavens falling in.
The frilled pool swallows.
Half-lit leaves become shards of a grand starlight.

So what happens next: only night?
Or a comet shear, god's requiem dray, a revelation?
Branches at the pool's rim whisk the owl-echoes
in a dying breeze, brindled watertint, coffee or chestnut
darkens to a moody mirror of his tracksore limbs.

Quietly he unpacks his food in the place of shroud & healing.
The feathered codes and liquid palates
lug then oxygenate his burden.
When the fire ignites the gumcrack & flare
casts whole nerve-galaxies into the background.
His heart-enclosure is rehoused for ballads.
His squeezebox is breathing.
The bug-eyes of night-souls gain a reedy companion.

Anytime Before Byzantium

From the back deck I hear the swans cry
look up, and see them winging by.
Each of them contains two motifs:
the curlicue **2** when on the water
the eelneck & bodybulb when on the air.
That outsretched neck, the strange ungainly,
makes them a miracle polytemporal
as when I see them flying at night
with a moon of hammered gold behind
flying as if in oil paint in 1865
or on a cup embossed in 1265
or anytime before Byzantium or through
the reed architecture of Iraq, or above
and beyond the eel-weirs of here.
The eyes transport – they are boats –
the ears inspire – they fill the lungs –
but if perchance you only see the gleam of screens
this most natural yet tutelary of spirits
would seem as freakish as a normal baby born
or the real and everyday vanishment of death.
Art's 'surreal black swan' is obviously our own doing
while the swan flying-on governs its own presentation.

Grace then is when the palette of habitat
blends with our inner picture of its creatures.
The bird glides from sepia-wet, enters the ink of dune-shadow
which in turn blends into incomparable night.

The swan is rubbed away but we know it is still there
dreaming under the wing. It is our memory
that shines the star. Without it we are blank
and the night is never that.

Keep the swan in your heart, the workaday
of its paddling feet, the glamour of its buoyant glide.
This is the inclusiveness of swan, the classlessness of brackish light
the ethics of how we are more than one.
Listen, through life's mindless tunes until
you know its voice like a wild relative.
Then, on the back deck, in an auditorium of estuary
or on the pavement grey, smile.
But take no direction from me
nor any other baton of the historical score,
go out under your own dream-wing
swim the river beyond time to find
the sound and texture of water.

Acknowledgements

Special thanks go to the local readers of many of these poems, Sian Marlow, Antoinette Hanna, John Clarke and Amanda Johnson. Their insight and expertise has been invaluable. Thanks too to my publisher Barry Scott and my agent Jeanne Ryckmans for their faith, support and good humour. I'd also like to thank the editors of the anthologies, newspapers and magazines in which some of these poems have appeared previously: *Australian Love Poems*, *Ecopoetics*, *Australian Poetry Journal*, *The Age*, *The Saturday Paper*, *The Weekend Australian.*

The epigram from Dante's Divine Comedy at the beginning of the book is from the Robin Kirkpatrick translation of Canto XVIII of Paradiso. The quote from Seamus Heaney at the beginning of Grass Tree School is from his Nobel Lecture, Crediting Poetry. Aside from place names, occasional Wadawurrung words in the poems are versions from the Wadawurrung language app, a valuable resource made generously available online by the Wadawurrung traditional owners. 'a stór' is Irish for 'my treasure'. 'fiumare' is an Italian word for river. In Dante's Inferno, 'contrapasso' is the punishment of souls in a way that either resembles or directly contrasts with the sin itself. 'noli timere' is Latin for 'don't be afraid'. 'Je me souviens' (I remember) and 'Les Choses' (Things) are both titles of books by Georges Perec.

Two of the sequences in this collection, Visitors and A Smile At Arm's Length, were previously published as fine artist-books, in 2012 and 2016 respectively, in limited editions of 12 copies, in collaboration with Jiri Tibor Novak and Sian Marlow.